Twelfth Night

William Shakespeare

Guide written by
John Mahoney

A *Letts* Literature Guide

Every effort has been made to trace copyright holders and to obtain their permission for the use of copyright material. The author and publishers will gladly receive information enabling them to rectify any reference or credit in subsequent editions.

First published 1994
Reprinted 1994

Letts Educational
Aldine House
Aldine Place
London W12 8AW

Text © John Mahoney and Stewart Martin 1994

Typeset by Jordan Publishing Design

Self-test questions devised by Claire Wright

Text design Jonathan Barnard

Cover and text illustrations Hugh Marshall

Graphic illustration Ian Foulis and Associates, Barbara Linton

Design © BPP (Letts Educational) Ltd

ISBN 1 85758 248 9

British Library Cataloguing in Publication Data
A CIP record for this book is available from the British Library.

Printed and bound in Great Britain by
Ashford Colour Press Ltd, Gosport, Hants

Letts Educational is the trading name of BPP (Letts Educational) Ltd

Contents

▓ Plot synopsis

Viola and Sebastian, identical twins, are shipwrecked on the shore of Illyria, a land ruled by the Duke of Orsino.

Viola, thinking her brother has probably drowned but hoping that he is still alive, decides to seek her fortune. The Captain of her ship, who also escaped drowning, tells her that the Duke of Orsino is a bachelor, and that the Countess Olivia, who is currently wooed by the Duke, is in mourning. Like Viola, Olivia has lost a brother and she is determined to mourn his loss for some years.

Disguising herself as a man and using the name Cesario, Viola seeks employment with Orsino. The Duke likes this young 'man', Cesario, and gives him the duty of telling Olivia how much he loves her. Olivia, however, does not love Orsino and will not accept his advances. Instead, she takes a liking to Cesario, and falls in love with 'him', much to Viola's embarrassment. However, the other complication is that Viola has fallen in love with Orsino.

Having survived the shipwreck too, Sebastian, Viola's twin brother, arrives in Illyria, with Antonio, the captain of the ship which rescued him. Sir Andrew Aguecheek, a rejected suitor of Olivia, challenges Cesario to a duel because he thinks Olivia favours 'him'. Cesario is rescued by Antonio, who thinks he is Sebastian. Antonio is then arrested for an old crime and claims from Cesario a purse which he had lent to Sebastian. Cesario denies him the purse, and Antonio is taken to prison.

Olivia, thinking Sebastian is Cesario, asks him to marry her. To her delight, he agrees. Orsino arrives and discovers that his man Cesario appears to have betrayed him by marrying Olivia. However, when both Viola and Sebastian appear together, the mystery is solved. Orsino, on discovering that Cesario is in fact a woman, can allow his admiration and love for Viola to surface, and they marry.

A subplot concerns Olivia's uncle, Sir Toby Belch and her steward, Malvolio. Sir Toby is a drunkard and his revels annoy Malvolio, who is serious and self-important. Sir Toby, with the help of Olivia's maid Maria, hatches a plot to make Malvolio look foolish. They forge a letter from Olivia to Malvolio which suggests that she loves him. Malvolio is taken in by the letter, makes amorous approaches to Olivia, and is imprisoned as a madman for his pains. Eventually the trick is explained to Olivia, and Malvolio is released, though he does not forgive the pranksters and vows revenge. Sir Toby marries Maria.

Characters and themes

Viola

The character who links all the action of the play is Viola who, disguised as a man, takes the name Cesario. She is resourceful, determined and courageous.

Olivia

Olivia, in mourning for her brother, is determined to reject the advances of Duke Orsino as she does not love him. But her determination to mourn her brother does not last long when Cesario arrives. Olivia falls in love with him. As she commands and runs a large household, she is well thought of.

Orsino

Orsino, the local Duke, is very much in love with the *idea* of being in love with Olivia. However, it is really Viola, disguised as Cesario, who catches his eye and whom he eventually marries.

Sebastian

Sebastian, like his sister, is resourceful and courageous, and he is also impulsive – witness his sudden decision to marry Olivia.

Major themes

There are four major themes. One is disguise, or the difficulty of distinguishing between appearance and reality. The problems which arise from mistaken identities, especially those of Viola and Sebastian, form the backbone of the plot. Disorder, another theme, is apparent in the drunken revels of Sir Toby, in his misuse of Sir Andrew's friendship and money, and in his persecution of Malvolio. This theme acts almost as a counterpoint to the main action. Love is another major theme with the play being the story of two love affairs: that of Orsino and Viola, and that of Olivia and Sebastian. This theme incorporates the misplaced love of Sir Andrew and Malvolio for Olivia, as well as the eventual marriage of Sir Toby and Maria. Finally, music as a theme supports the theme of love. It is, in Orsino's words, 'the food of love', with the play beginning and ending with music.

Plot and subplot

The main plot concerns the love entanglements between Viola, Orsino, Olivia and Sebastian. They are made more complicated by the disguise adopted by Viola and the fact that she and her brother, Sebastian, are identical twins. The subplot concerns the fooling of Malvolio, Olivia's steward, by Sir Toby and Olivia's maid Maria.

ORSINO	VIOLA	OLIVIA	SEBASTIAN	SUBPLOT
				**Act One**
Orsino tells of his love for Olivia: 'If music be the food of love...'	Shipwrecked, Viola, in disguise, will seek her fortune:	Olivia rejects Orsino and will mourn her dead brother: 'Like a cloistress veiled walk'	Viola's twin brother, 'most provident in peril', might have been saved	Olivia condemns Malvolio: 'O, you are sick of self-love'
Orsino has confided in Viola: 'I have unclasped to thee the book even of my secret soul'	'What else may hap to this I will commit'	Viola courts Olivia for Orsino: 'Make me a willow cabin at your gate'.... 'Olivia falls in love with Viola: 'This youth's perfections... creep in at mine eyes'		
	Viola has fallen in love with Orsino: 'Whoe'er I woo, myself would be his wife'			**Act Two**
			Sebastian, thinking his sister is dead, determines to go to Orsino's court	Sir Toby rebukes Malvolio: 'Shall there be no more cakes and ale?'
Viola loves Orsino but is duty bound to woo Olivia for him				Maria plots Malvolio's downfall

Act Three

Act Four

Act Five

Malvolio reads the letter: 'Some are born great…'

Malvolio, in ridiculous dress and manners, 'woos' Olivia and is imprisoned

Released from prison
Malvolio vows revenge

Sir Andrew strikes Sebastian
Sir Toby intervenes
Olivia intervenes

Olivia proposes to Sebastian – he accepts: 'Wouldst thou be ruled by me!'

Olivia and Sebastian: 'You are betrothed both to a man and a maid'

Orsino thinks he loves Olivia, and finds Viola attractive

Viola 'duels' Sir Andrew
Antonio defends 'Sebastian'

Olivia declares her love fro Viola: 'Love sought is good, but given unsought is better – and rejected'

Orsino and Viola: 'Give me thy hand, and let me see thee in thy woman's weeds'

The disguised Viola is unmasked: 'One face, one voice, one habit, and two persons!'

'Thus the whirligig of time brings in his revenge'

Viola

Viola

'She bore a mind that envy could not but call fair' (Act 2 Sc 1). This was Sebastian's assessment of his sister Viola, and it is perhaps the most accurate of all, despite the fact that the speaker is undoubtedly biased in her favour.

We first meet Viola in the second scene of Act 1. She has survived a shipwreck, but believes her brother may have died in the wreck. When told by the Captain that a local lady, Olivia, has also recently suffered the loss of a brother, she briefly wonders whether to join her in a period of mourning. However, her common sense soon reasserts itself, and she sets her mind to making the best of her situation.

Learning from the Captain that the local governor is called Orsino, the Duke of Illyria, she determines to seek him out and gain employment with him. Being a woman in a foreign land, she decides she will be safer if she disguises herself as a man. Then she lists her talents: 'I can sing/ And speak...in many sorts of music' (Act 1 Sc 2) and shows she has real accomplishments.

Thus she shows a great deal of practical thinking, swift decision-making and a business-like manner. You might contrast her reaction to the loss of a brother with that of Olivia. Viola is not certain her brother is dead, but she is determined to carry on and hope that perhaps he might have survived.

Because of her sensible approach to matters, she is well able to make judgements about situations and to decide when she cannot affect an outcome:

'O time, thou must untangle this, not I.
It is too hard a knot for me to untie!'

2, 2

Aware that Olivia has fallen in love with her in the guise of Cesario, she recognises that there is nothing she can do at that moment to make things right.

She is persistent and determined in the execution of her duties for the Duke. On her first visit to Olivia, she manages to talk her way into Olivia's presence. She is also loyal to the point of ignoring her own best interests. Even when she realises that she has fallen in love with Orsino, she decides to carry on with her mission to win Olivia on Orsino's behalf.

'...I'll do my best

To woo your lady. Yet, a barful strife!

Whoe'er I woo, myself would be his wife.'

1, 4

This sense of loyalty and tact extends to others, as when she keeps secret from Malvolio Olivia's ploy of sending her a ring. It would not do for Malvolio to realise his mistress was chasing after a mere messenger. Her concern for others extends even to her purse. She does not know Antonio when, confusing her with Sebastian, he claims he loaned her money, but even so she offers him half her purse.

As a woman she is also sensitive to her physical weakness. She is not happy at the thought of taking part in a duel, but nevertheless, though tempted, does not throw off her disguise: 'A little thing would make me tell them how much I lack of a man' (3, 4). She is also easily deceived by Sir Toby and Fabian, and in this sense is not too 'wordly wise'.

That she impresses others is clear. The Duke takes her into his confidence and admires her beauty: 'Diana's lip/ Is not more smooth and rubious' (1, 4). Even the dour Malvolio calls her 'well-favoured' (1, 5) and Sir Andrew calls her 'a rare courtier' (3, 1).

Perhaps Viola's one error of judgement might be seen as her love for the languid Orsino, Duke of Illyria. Their characters and personalities seem so different that the audience might wonder if she is wise in her choice of man. But, then, he does have positive characteristics of his own. Her character commends itself to the audience. She gains their sympathy from the outset and retains it throughout the play.

Olivia

As the other major female character in the play, it is inevitable that we should contrast Olivia with Viola. To some extent their circumstances are the same. Both are obviously well bred and come from well-to-do families. Both have recently suffered the loss of a brother. Olivia's died soon after the death of her father, some twelve months before the play opens. Yet

Olivia

their reactions to their losses are totally different. Olivia has decided to stay in mourning for seven years, and in remembrance:

> 'like a cloistress she will veiled walk,
> And water once a day her chamber round
> With eye-offending brine…'

1, 1

This is an affected and unrealistic pose, but perhaps we should remember that she is young and has lost, it would seem, all her family within twelve months. The excesses of youth may well excuse her attitude. That it is not deep-rooted is seen by the speed with which she abandons her mourning when a desirable young man in the form of Cesario arrives.

The Captain, a source of much information, describes her as 'fair Olivia' and a 'virtuous maid' (1, 2). Orsino suggests that 'heaven walks on earth' (5, 1) when Olivia enters.

Viola has much opportunity to know Olivia and gives this account of her: '…you are too proud:/But if you were the devil, you are fair.' (1, 5). Sebastian, even on his short acquaintance with Olivia, makes a shrewd judgement about her capabilities. He tells how she:

> 'sway(s) her house, command(s) her followers,
> Take(s) and give(s) back affairs and their dispatch,
> With such a smooth, discrete, and stable bearing'

4, 3

He finds her impressive, and her capabilities as well as her position and beauty obviously contribute to the swiftness with which he decides to accept her offer of marriage – note, *she* proposes to *him*. Her determination to pursue Cesario's hand in marriage and her willingness to make the first move say much for her strong and resolute character.

Olivia's own words and actions also give evidence of her character and capabilities. She judges character well, both of her servants and of Orsino. She recognises that the Duke's declaration is false: 'it is heresy' (1, 5). She tells Cesario that Orsino already knows her mind and she is quite emphatic in her rejection of him. Whilst valuing Malvolio's services, she also knows his weaknesses: 'O, you are sick of self-love, Malvolio' (1, 5), but she can also be sensitive to the hurt that has been done him and desires that he shall be sure of gaining justice for his sufferings: 'Thou shalt be both the plaintiff and the judge/Of thine own cause.' (5, 1)

Perhaps we might judge her as impetuous when so soon after meeting Cesario she decides she must woo and marry him. But equally we can see her as a woman of decision who knows her own mind.

Orsino

Orsino

Again the Captain's words are apt when it comes to describing Orsino's underlying characteristics: 'A noble Duke, in nature as in name' (1, 2). This is a judgement we need to keep in mind when considering the way he is first presented.

He has a love for music that is plain from his opening words, but that love is bound up with the melancholy air he has when speaking of his love for Olivia: 'If music be the food of love, play on' (1, 1). It seems to be a pose: he is in love with the idea of being in love, and Olivia, with her decision to keep herself pure for seven years, is an ideal object for his unrealistic love. As Duke of Illyria, he could easily bestir himself and visit Olivia, but he seems to prefer to conduct his love-making from a distance, and through Cesario. Olivia sees through his pose: she calls his love for her a 'heresy' (1, 5).

He appears to be a very languid and affected man, unlike Sebastian with whom we inevitably compare him. Compared to Viola, he is positively slothful! Note that it is not until the very end of the play that he makes the decision to visit Olivia, when his presence is required to further the action. He quickly recognises that he does not really desire Olivia, but loves Viola once her real identity is known.

However, his positive attributes are recognised. Olivia, whilst rejecting his love, says of him:

'I suppose him virtuous, know him noble,
Of great estate, of fresh and stainless youth,
in voices well divulged, free, learned, and valiant,
And in dimension and the shape of nature
A gracious person...'

1, 5

One could not ask for a more positive testimony.

Feste, another good judge of character, suggests the Duke has a changeable nature when he says Orsino's tailor should make his 'doublet of changeable taffeta, for thy mind is a very opal' (2, 4).

Orsino's words to Cesario, when he thinks he has been

betrayed, are fierce: 'I'll sacrifice the lamb that I do love,/To spite a raven's heart within a dove.' (5, 1), as is the way he describes his love for Olivia: 'as hungry as the sea' (2, 4). There is a hint here of a very different character. He ably rules his country, and we learn both from himself and from Antonio that he has taken part in battle:

'That face of his I do remember well.
Yet when I saw it last, it was besmeared
As black as Vulcan in the smoke of war.'

5, 1

At times the language he uses at the end of the play is in stark contrast to that he uses at the beginning: 'Kill what I love? – savage jealousy...tear out of that cruel eye...my thoughts are ripe in mischief' (5, 1), and point towards a very different man than is suggested by his languid and relaxed pose.

He can be gracious and forgiving and recognise a fierce adversary, as when he comments admiringly how Antonio captured the best of his ships so that 'very envy and the tongue of loss/Cried fame and honour on him' (5, 1).

However, in the end the audience may well judge that his seemingly languid nature and his affected pose on the matter of his love for Olivia do not make him a very attractive hero or lover. Is he worthy of Viola? She obviously thinks so, and perhaps we should accept her judgement!

Sebastian

It is, again, the Captain's testimony at the very beginning of the play which sets out Sebastian's major characteristics:

'...I saw your brother,
Most provident in peril, bind himself –
Courage and hope both teaching him the practice–'

1, 2

'Provident in peril', 'courageous' and 'hopeful' also describes Viola's character, and underlines the fact that, in character as well as looks, she is her brother's identical twin. This is an important consideration for the furtherance of the plot, for when Sebastian arrives on the scene, his similarity to Cesario, both in appearance and in action, ensures the various episodes of mistaken identity can smoothly take their place on the stage.

Sebastian demonstrates good judgement of Viola's appearance and character: she 'was yet of many accounted beautiful' and 'she bore a mind that envy could not but call fair.' (2, 1). He also shows consideration for Antonio, trying to ensure that Antonio does not put himself in danger by accompanying him to Orsino's court. However, Antonio's insistence shows what a high regard he has for Sebastian. Equally, when they arrive in the town Antonio's willingness to give him his purse confirms both his love for and trust of Sebastian. Antonio's actions suggest that Sebastian must be a very worthy character to inspire such trust and affection.

Sebastian is very much a man of action. When confronted by Sir Andrew's unprovoked attack, he responds swiftly and is willing to take Sir Toby on as well, giving an excellent account of himself. That swiftness of action and ability to judge people stands him in good stead when he meets Olivia. Startled by his reception, he nevertheless reacts quickly. He judges Olivia to be worthy, capable and beautiful, and agrees to marry her.

His reaction to Antonio when they at last meet again is obviously genuine; he has been searching for his friend and is very pleased to see him again:

> 'Antonio! O, my dear Antonio!
> How have the hours racked and tortured me
> Since I have lost thee!'
>
> 5, 1

When he pledges his love to Olivia,

> 'And having sworn truth, ever will be true.'
>
> 4, 3

we feel he will be as good as his word.

Sir Toby Belch

Unlike the characters looked at so far, Sir Toby is a man of contradictions. His last name, Belch, is a good indicator of his personality, for it sums up his drunken, overlarge nature in a particularly unflattering way. He lives down to his name very efficiently.

Virtually every time we meet him in the play he is drinking and enjoying himself. His rejection of all that Malvolio seems to stand for:

> 'Dost thou think, because thou art virtuous, there shall be no more cakes and ale?'
>
> 2, 3

sums up his attitude. In a similar vein, his assertion in the very first lines he speaks: 'I am sure care's an enemy to life' (1, 3) supports the view that he is a drunken old reveller. However, this is too simplistic a judgement of him.

That he is quick-witted is seen in his conversations with Sir Andrew, Maria, Feste and Malvolio, in which he holds his own, with swift repartee. He is aware that he may have gone too far in the plot against Malvolio and ensures that Malvolio is released before Olivia is sufficiently enraged to turn her uncle out of her house. He shows good judgement of character when he correctly guesses that Cesario has no stomach for a duel with Sir Andrew. He also recognises Maria's sterling qualities, and finally marries her.

There is, however, also a downside to his character, apart from his drunken revels. His comments about Maria: 'She's a beagle true bred, and one that adores me – what o'that?' (2, 3) suggest self-satisfaction and lack of respect for her. The callous way he treats Sir Andrew in taking his money under pretext of advancing his cause with Olivia, and in making fun of him both to his face and behind his back do not endear him to us. Also the way he treats Malvolio – it is his idea to have him locked up as a madman – shows that he has a cruel side.

In the end, however, he represents the low comedy of *Twelfth Night*. As such he generates much of the play's humour and energy and provides a contrast to the courtly love affairs of the main plot.

Sir Andrew Aguecheek

For once it is not the Captain who provides information on a character, but Maria. She says of Sir Andrew:

> '...he's a fool, he's a great quarreller; and but that he hath the gift of a coward to allay the gust he hath in quarrelling, 'tis thought among the prudent he would quickly have the gift of a grave.'
>
> 1, 3

A fool, a coward and a quarreller – not a flattering portrait, but then Sir Andrew does not appear to be a very attractive character at all. Sir Toby says that Sir Andrew can speak 'three or four languages word for word without book', but this is more of a criticism than a compliment, suggesting that he has merely learned a number of foreign phrases by heart, in order to show off. Certainly his conversation shows little expertise in English, let alone in other languages.

In his foolishness he blindly follows everything Sir Toby suggests and believes everything he says. On the one occasion he makes a sensible suggestion, that Sir Toby would have gained the best of the duel if he had not been drunk, the reward he gets from Sir Toby is to be called 'An asshead, and a coxcomb, and a knave – a thin-faced knave, a gull!' (5, 1). Such insults he has endured before, but his foolishness is shown in other ways as well.

The ease with which Sir Toby parts him from his money shows him to be a fool, and the fact that he believes Olivia might choose him for her husband shows him to be foolish indeed. Sir Toby's words quoted above are perhaps the best description of Sir Andrew Aguecheek. However, he serves a useful purpose in the play. He is a foil for Sir Toby, in words, appearance and action. His foolish love for Olivia parallels Malvolio's similar foolish hope. His cowardly attack on frightened Cesario and then on not-so-frightened Sebastian provide moments of humour and light relief.

Feste (Sir Topas)

Feste

As the one person who moves freely between all groupings of characters, and between main and subplot, Feste is ideally placed both to comment on the action and to help it along. The professional fool of the play, as distinct from 'real' fools like Sir Andrew and Malvolio, he observes that:

> 'Foolery, sir, does walk about the orb like the sun, it shines everywhere.'

3, 1

– and so he does indeed 'shine everywhere'.

But perhaps Feste is most associated with music. Whether singing love songs for Orsino or revels for Sir Toby, his love of music comes across clearly. What he has to say in his songs is also important. His song in Act 2 Sc 3, although a love song for Sir Toby, clearly also refers to the action of the main plot: 'Present mirth hath present laughter;/What's to come is still unsure:'

He is a shrewd commentator on character and action. He takes Olivia to task for the time she intends to spend in mourning for her brother, 'proving' the folly of her actions:

'The more fool, madonna, to mourn for your brother's soul, being in heaven' (1, 5). His comments about the Duke's mind being like 'taffeta...and opal' (2, 4) sum up aspects of Orsino's character. Of Sir Andrew he comments: 'Better a witty fool than a foolish wit' (1, 5). Of the drunken Sir Toby he says: 'the fool shall look to the madman' (1, 5). In his conversation with the imprisoned Malvolio he prophetically declares that Malvolio will 'remain...in darkness' (4, 2); not simply the darkness of the room but of Malvolio's own mind: at the end Malvolio's last words are a vow of revenge against those who have harmed him, rather than a realisation of where his own folly has led him.

Perhaps it falls to Viola to sum up Feste accurately:

> 'This fellow is wise enough to play the fool;
> And to do that well craves a kind of wit.
> ...As full of labour as a wise man's art,
> For folly that he wisely shows is fit;'

> 3, 1

viola

He plays the fool well, but he is no fool.

Malvolio

Malvolio

Malvolio creates a range of responses in our minds. On the one hand he is a most unlovable, pretentious character; on the other he has our sympathy for the way he is treated by Sir Toby and Maria. He is a Puritan, a person with excessively strict views about morality. A man of his views is bound to come into conflict with Sir Toby.

Olivia values his services as a steward and when she comes to the conclusion that he is ill, she commands: 'Let some of my people have a special care of him: I would not have him miscarry for the half of my dowry' (3, 4). At an earlier stage she leaves matters in his hands when Viola seeks entrance:

> 'if it be a suit from the Count, I am sick, or not at home
> – what you will, to dismiss it.'

> 5, 1

– she obviously values his services and trusts his judgement.

Olivia does, however, recognise his major failing, one that Maria takes full advantage of in the subplot: 'O, you are sick of self-love, Malvolio, and taste with a distempered appetite.' (1, 5), and it is Sir Toby who develops the image of appetite by suggesting that just because Malvolio is full of 'virtue', that is no reason why there should be no more 'cakes and ale'. It is also Maria who puts his foolish streak of self-love into clear language:

> 'the best persuaded of himself, so crammed, as he thinks, with excellencies, that it is his grounds of faith that all that look on him, love him – and on that vice in him will my revenge find notable cause to work.'
>
> 2, 3

and this is perhaps why he cannot get on with the servants, Sir Toby, or Maria. It also goes some way to explain his churlish behaviour to Viola when he throws Olivia's ring on the ground, and his very foolish view that he might one day be Olivia's husband: even before he received the letter he was playing out that particular fantasy.

No doubt we feel some sympathy, at times, for the man. But he leaves the audience struggling not to laugh at his misfortunes. His failure to recognise the ridiculous postures he has adopted, the extent to which he brought trouble on himself and the fact that he hasn't the humanity to be able to laugh at himself at the end of the play, alienate the audience.

Maria

As maid to Olivia, Maria shows early on in the play that she is aware that Sir Toby's revels could lead him into trouble with his niece. However, Maria's major contribution to the action is in devising the plan to make a fool of Malvolio. As such, she contributes to the humour and comic success of the subplot.

She can be sharp-tongued, as when she greets Viola (1, 5), and when she takes delight in making fun of Sir Andrew (1, 3). However, her devising of the plot against Malvolio shows her at her best. She thinks of the plot, she writes the letter, and she ensures that Malvolio will find it. She also devises the contents of the letter. It is Maria in Act 4 Sc 2 who suggests that Feste should disguise himself as Sir Topas the curate, to confuse Malvolio even more.

Fabian

Fabian does not have an important part in the plot, but he serves some useful purposes. He tells how Malvolio got him into trouble by reporting him to Olivia for bear-baiting, and thus helps to prejudice the audience against Malvolio. He is among those who watch Malvolio being tricked.

At the end of the play he lies to Olivia about who devised the plot against Malvolio, saying that Maria wrote the letter at Sir Toby's bidding. Thus he saves her from Olivia's wrath – she can less easily discipline Sir Toby than she can Maria. It is Fabian who tells the assembled company that Maria is now related to Olivia, as she has married Sir Toby.

Antonio

Antonio has a small but important part in the play. His friendship with Sebastian is such that he is willing to risk his freedom, life and purse for him. He is a courageous fighter: of his exploits as sea, Orsino says: 'very envy and the tongue of loss/Cried fame and honour on him.' He is on hand to rescue Cesario from the duel with Sir Andrew, and enables Viola to show herself generous to a stranger when she offers him half her purse.

The Captain

It is the Captain who aids Viola at the start of the play and he provides excellent background information about where the play is set. He also sketches in essential details of Orsino and Olivia, commenting accurately on their characters. He gives Viola hope that her brother is alive, describing how he saw him attempting to save himself.

■ Themes in *Twelfth Night*

Themes are the important ideas that run through the play. You will come across them many times. They connect the story, the characters and the different scenes in the play.

When words and descriptions suggest a picture in your mind, that is called an image. Images are often used to make an idea stronger, or to encourage you to think of things from a particular point of view. If you described someone as being 'as skinny as a stick' or as behaving 'like a wild animal' you would be using simple examples of images.

Shakespeare was a very great writer who used themes and images all the time. Many of the examples you will find are very striking and impressive. Other examples will be less obvious, so you will need to pay careful attention to the language that Shakespeare used. Read the following notes carefully.

Disguise

Disguise

This encompasses the themes of appearance and reality and mistaken identity. The disguise which leads to most confusion in the play is, of course, that of Viola when she dresses as a man and calls herself Cesario.

Viola's disguise does indeed fool everyone. Orsino is taken in, though he does make reference to Cesario's appearance, commenting on 'his' pleasing looks and youth. Olivia is so taken in by Viola's disguise that she falls in love with Cesario and wants to marry 'him'. At the end of the play even Sebastian, Viola's brother, cannot quite believe his eyes and needs her to recount details from their childhood to prove her identity.

If it were a simple matter of Viola being disguised as a man there would be confusion enough but, because she is identical to her twin brother Sebastian, other mistakes follow.

Sebastian is mistakenly identified as Cesario on a number of occasions. Feste, in Act 4 Sc 1, having been sent by Olivia to bring Cesario to her, finds Sebastian instead. His waylaying of Sebastian provides the opportunity for Sir Toby and Sir Andrew to arrive and also mistake him for Cesario. From their decision to engage him in a duel and the subsequent arrival of Olivia comes the opportunity for the mistake Olivia makes. She too, sees Sebastian and thinks he is Cesario. Much to her surprise, Sebastian is willing to accord to her desires (unlike Cesario) and so the scene is set for the final moments of the play.

Viola's disguise fools everyone, Sebastian is mistaken for Cesario, and more confusion follows when Cesario is mistaken for Sebastian. Antonio berates Cesario for rejecting him after all the trouble and danger he had gone to on his behalf. The priest, in confirming Sebastian's marriage to Olivia, declares that Cesario was the person he married to Olivia.

There are two other incidents of mistaken identity, and both involve Malvolio. Malvolio cannot see through the disguise of Feste when he pretends to be Sir Topas, the curate. Given the darkness of the room and the fact that Feste changes his voice this is not, perhaps, remarkable. The other matter is of more importance. Malvolio fails to see through the forged handwriting of the letter Maria wrote. She disguises her handwriting to look like Olivia's, and Malvolio is completely fooled.

Thus disguise is essential to both the main and subplot. Viola's disguise in the main plot leads to various confusions of the main plot, and in the subplot Malvolio is taken in by disguised handwriting and directly from that event comes his downfall.

Other things in the play are also disguised. Both Olivia and Orsino seem to be disguising their true feelings and personalities at the start of the play. Orsino is in love with the idea of being in love. He certainly does not appear to be, or have the potential to be, the man of action that reports of the sea battle against Antonio's pirate ship indicate. Olivia is attracted by the notion of mourning her dead brother for many years. That it is really an affectation is seen by the speed with which she turns her attention to Cesario.

Another major character also disguises her feelings. Viola, in the guise of Cesario, takes service with Orsino. She rapidly falls in love with him but this creates a real problem for her. Her duty is to woo Olivia on his behalf, and she remains true to her duty, disguising her true feelings in order to do so. Whilst she is aware of the confusion her disguise causes Olivia, she knows that to declare her true sex would expose her to danger – this is the reason she adopted the disguise. She is left with no alternative but to hide her true feelings and leave it to time to resolve the matter.

Another minor aspect of this theme relates to the feelings that Sir Toby and Maria have for each other. Always understated if not disguised, their love eventually surfaces, and they marry.

Love

Love and friendship

The play is about love but, fitting with the theme of mistaken identity, love comes in many guises.

Orsino

Orsino and love

Orsino says he is in love with Olivia, but she calls it a 'heresy' (i.e. a lie). He says:

> 'If music be the food of love, play on,
> Give me excess of it, that, surfeiting,
> The appetite may sicken, and so die.'
>
> 1, 1

This is a strange request. Orsino is asking, if music is the food of love, to be provided with an excessive amount so that eventually his appetite for the 'food of love' may 'die', and with it, presumably, love. It is a pose. He enjoys music, enjoys the thought of being in love, and he wants the emotional enjoyment of both, but his love is not realistic. Olivia is merely a totem, representing the idealised object of his love. His romantic love lacks a real object and is therefore superficial. His suggestion to Cesario in Act 2 Sc 4 that women are incapable of giving back to him the same passion and love as he can give them is ironic, as Viola loves him passionately. Orsino's 'love' for Olivia is false. But what of his love for Viola?

Viola quickly gains a place at his side and becomes Orsino's confidante: 'I have unclasped/To thee the book even of my secret soul' (1, 4). He admires Cesario's beauty: 'Diana's lip/ Is not more smooth and rubious' (1, 4), and his promise to Cesario that he may 'call his (Orsino's) fortunes thine' has an ironic though prophetic truth. He quizzes Cesario closely in Act 2 Scene 4 about love and whether 'he' is in love. Perhaps there is an element here of not wanting to lose Cesario's service.

Finally, Orsino goes to plead his cause directly with Olivia. Her curt rejection of him causes some pain and anger and his speech is much more forceful, his language more brutal than before. He ends by threatening to 'sacrifice the lamb that I do love' (5, 1), his first overt reference to affection for Cesario. This is quickly overturned when he realises Cesario is a woman, and then he recognises the true meaning of those 'thousand times' when Cesario said to him 'Thou never shouldst love woman like to me' (5, 1). Now, Orsino is really in love.

Olivia and love

Olivia

Olivia's love for her brother is, much like Orsino's love for her, false. Not in the sense that she does not really grieve his loss, but in that her vow to mourn for seven years, her sprinkling of the chamber with tears, and her wearing of a veil, are all pure theatricals, empty gestures that say nothing about her true grief. Perhaps the only real purpose they serve is to keep Orsino's own theatrical display of love at a distance!

However, the love she shows for Cesario is another matter. From the moment she first sets eyes on 'him' in Act 1 Sc 5, Olivia is in love. It must otherwise strike one as a little strange that, after hearing of Cesario's mission and then seeing 'him' she should send away her attendants – surely this is not to welcome loving messages from Orsino, a man she rejects outright? Having sent away her people, she quickly agrees to unveil her face. It is as though she makes herself open and welcoming to Cesario. Swiftly rejecting Orsino's declarations of love, Olivia is far more concerned to know about Cesario, for twice she asks about 'his' parentage. When Cesario leaves, Olivia sends a ring after 'him' by Malvolio, an excuse to tempt 'him' back. There can be no doubt of the strength of Olivia's love, even at this early stage. In Act 3, she declares her love for Cesario:

'Love sought, is good; but given unsought, is better.'

3, 1

Unfortunately for Olivia the love she seeks, Cesario's, is not for her. The love she gives unsought is not accepted. She is rejected, just as she has rejected the Duke. She quizzes Cesario on 'his' opinion of her, desperate for a sign of affection or love but all she thinks she sees is 'a deal of scorn (that) looks beautiful/In the contempt and anger of his lip!' (3, 1). It is perhaps a mark of true love that no amount of rejection will ever quench the blaze. Eager to see Cesario again, Olivia even holds out the false promise that Cesario might, if 'he' returns, 'move/That heart, which now abhors, to like his (Orsino's) love' (3, 1).

In contrast to Orsino's leisurely pursuit of her from a distance, Olivia sends for Cesario. In her anxiety she actually debases her own true love by suggesting that: 'youth is bought more oft than begged or borrowed' (3, 4) and wonders what she can 'bestow' (i.e. give) him to buy his love. She offers a jewel, and gains Cesario's promise to come again.

Given the intensity of Olivia's love, it is no surprise that when she mistakes Sebastian for Cesario and hears the words she has dreamed of – 'Madam, I will (be ruled by you)' (4, 1) – she loses absolutely no time in sealing the promise.

Viola and love

Viola

Of the three major characters who occupy much of the play, Viola's love is the most balanced and controlled. She loves her brother dearly but, unlike Olivia, Viola has neither the time nor the inclination to spend seven years in mourning. She briefly considers joining Olivia in her grief: 'O that I served that lady/And might not be delivered to the world' (1, 2). However, Viola is both active and realistic, and determines to seek her fortune at Orsino's court.

Like her brother, she falls in love suddenly and, like Olivia, the love she seeks is not returned. Not for her are the flights of romantic poetry so beloved of Orsino, or the forward declarations of love favoured by Olivia. She recognises her love, but does her duty to the man who is employing her: 'I'll do my best/To woo your lady' (1, 4) even though she (Viola) would rather be his wife.

Her conversations with Olivia are dignified and beyond reproach in terms of the duty she owes Orsino. The intensity of the love she has for him is seen when she explains to Olivia how she would go in pursuit of her love:

> 'Make me a willow cabin at your gate,
> And call upon my soul within the house;
> ...O, you should not rest
> Between the elements of air and earth,
> But you should pity me.'

>   1, 5

Unfortunately for Viola she is never in the position to declare her love openly.

It is Viola, who declares, with some insight: 'time, thou must untangle this, not I' (2, 2), and time indeed does. It rewards her hope that her brother might be alive and, at the same time, it gives her the opportunity to declare her love for Orsino.

Sebastian and love

Sebastian

Our first acquaintance with Sebastian is in Act 2 Sc 1. There we witness the unfettered friendship and love that he has inspired in Antonio and the love that he gives in return. This is no foolish, romantic liaison, but the recognition of admirable traits in each other's character and the wish to share in each other's pains and pleasures. That Sebastian holds Antonio dear is witnessed in Act 5:

> 'How have the hours racked and tortured me
> Since I have lost thee!'
>
> 5,1

His swift acceptance of Olivia's love and proposal of marriage is perhaps surprising, but remember he is a man of decision, a quality he shares with his sister. Thus his acceptance of Olivia and marriage do not really strike a discordant note.

Misguided love

Malvolio is the prime example here. In Olivia's words, he is 'sick of self-love'. His conceit is such that he is perfectly willing to believe Olivia is in love with him, and fools himself that the loves her. Maria's trick plays on his excessive self-love, making him an object of ridicule.

Sir Andrew also suffers from misguided love for Olivia. Sir Toby encourages Sir Andrew's courtship of his niece in order to keep him near as a source of money. One gets the distinct impression that, but for Sir Toby, he would have given up his pursuit of Olivia very easily.

Sir Toby and Maria

Maria's enthusiasm for 'gulling' Malvolio springs from the man's obnoxious personality, but no doubt she also feels it makes her a favourite of Sir Toby. It is Feste who first suggests that if Sir Toby had his wits about him he would look carefully at Maria (1, 5). Sir Toby on two occasions mentions Maria and love, but in an unromantic way, as perhaps befits 'Sir Belch'. However, it is in keeping with the play's major theme, love, that Sir Toby and Maria should also get married at the end.

Music

Music

>'If music be the food of love…'
>
>   1,1

Music is integral to the play's atmosphere. The atmosphere of many scenes is supported and enhanced by the music that accompanies them, whether it be the rarefied climate of Orsino's court, or the excited revelry of Sir Toby's merrymaking. The play begins with instrumental music and ends with a song. In virtually every scene, music is mentioned, played or sung.

Viola suggests that her musical ability may gain her entrance to the Duke's court and it does, as the Duke is fond of music. She says to Olivia that were she a suitor she would 'Write royal cantons of contemned love/And sing them loud even in the dead of night' (1, 5). Sir Toby's drunken revels are enlivened by music. Feste sings 'Hey Robin, jolly Robin' (4, 2) when he taunts Malvolio that 'she (Olivia) loves another'.

Feste sings three important songs in the play. The love song he sings for Sir Toby and Sir Andrew in Act 2 Sc 3 encourages the listener to grasp love whilst young, because 'what's to come is still unsure'. He also, prophetically, sings: 'Journeys end in lovers meeting' (2, 3). Both elements are relevant to the play's action and theme of love. Feste's next song, for Orsino, presents a tragic view of life and love which fits the Duke's mood: 'Come away, come away, death,…Sad true lover never find my grave to weep there!' (2, 4). Feste's last song is sung directly to the audience. He sings of the loveless life of a drunkard. It presents the reverse of the picture we have just witnessed and perhaps brings a little reality into the romantic idealism of this comedy.

Disorder

Disorder

In a very real sense the subplot, which deals with the fooling and imprisonment of Malvolio, acts as a counterpoint to the main plot. In the main plot we are concerned with higher things: the loves of Viola, Orsino, Olivia and Sebastian. The language and style of presentation supports the romantic atmosphere. In contrast, the subplot is a boisterous, disorderly revel. Even where the subplot mimics the main plot in terms of love affairs, disorder prevails. The antics of Malvolio and Sir Andrew are the antithesis of proper courtship. Even the one marriage in the subplot, of Sir Toby and Maria, seems to happen as if by chance, as an afterthought.

Malvolio is universally disliked by the servants, particularly by Sir Toby, Maria and Sir Andrew. He has annoyed Fabian, and Olivia too is irritated by his conceit. The conversations between the characters of the subplot are full of jibes and criticism. As such, they present a picture of disorder far from the world of the main plot.

There are also occasions within the play when order is threatened, either by violence or by misunderstanding and these spread across both main and subplots. A duel is arranged between Sir Andrew and Cesario which, if it happened, could be dangerous for both; Antonio is arrested in an enemy country; Sebastian is attacked by Sir Toby and Sir Andrew; Sir Toby, anxious to keep in Olivia's good books, needs Malvolio to be released, which Feste is in no hurry to do; Olivia thinks that Cesario has broken his vows to her; and Orsino believes he has been betrayed by Cesario. As well as these moments of tension, there is that element of conflict which comes with Olivia's continued rejection of Orsino. This undercurrent of violence threatens the apparent order and harmony of the main plot.

■ Text commentary

Act 1 Scene 1

A brief scene introducing Orsino, Duke of Illyria, who declares he is in love with Olivia, a local countess. The theme of music begins the play and its relationship to love is stressed. We learn that Olivia intends to mourn her brother for seven years.

'The food of love'

Music

Orsino

Music has an important role in the play because it is a backdrop to much of the action. Given that love is a major theme, music can, in Orsino's words, be 'the food of love'. The importance of music is emphasised by the fact that the play opens to the sound of musicians playing and closes with Feste's song: 'When that I was a little tiny boy'.

In the opening words of this first scene, Orsino speaks some of the most famous of Shakespeare's lines, lines which speak of the intensity of his love (for Olivia) and use the imagery of music as a food. The Duke's phrasing is rather artificial and his language is self-consciously flowery, which alert us to the fact that he *pretends* passion.

Love is the central theme of the play. Note how swiftly characters fall in love and, just as swiftly, marry.

> 'If music be the food of love, play on,
> Give me excess of it that, surfeiting,
> The appetite may sicken, and so die.'

You ought to know these lines by heart as far as the words '...as it was before.'

The words 'Even in a minute: so full of shapes in fancy/That it alone is high fantastical' give some indication that in matters of love, things are not always as they seem.

The reference to the sea in Orsino's first speech links with the events which follow, as it is the aftermath of the shipwreck involving Sebastian and Viola which gives rise to confusions of identity later in the play.

Unhappy Olivia

Having learned of Orsino's love for Olivia, we quickly discover that it has been rejected and that she intends to remain secluded for seven years, in remembrance of her dead brother. Such a length of mourning is excessive, but in a way it parallels

Olivia

that excess of love shown by Orsino. Keep their attitudes in mind when you meet Viola, and contrast her robust reaction to the loss of her brother.

Note how, in this first scene, later events and ideas are rehearsed: frustrated love, the death of a brother, the pervasive influence of music, reference to the sea that leads to the next scene, and the difference between appearance and reality – is Orsino *really* in love with Olivia, or does he only *think* he is? How real is Olivia's determination to mourn her dead brother for seven years? Are these two people disguising their true feelings? There is no simple answer at this stage, but seeds of doubt are sown here which are developed in later events.

Act 1 Scene 2

Viola is introduced, and we learn that her brother is possibly lost in the shipwreck which left her on the shores of Illyria. She is a stranger to Illyria and her questioning of the Captain ensures that the audience is given important background knowledge about the characters of the play. Viola determines to disguise herself as a man and enter the Duke's service, and that decision leads to the entanglements of the main plot.

Another brother lost?

Note how the death of Olivia's brother is mirrored here by the possible loss of Viola's brother, Sebastian. However, the Captain describes how, when he last saw Viola's brother, Sebastian was striving to save himself. Thus there is hope that he, like Viola, might have survived the shipwreck.

The ship's captain sketches in for Viola, and the audience, the affairs of Illyria with regard to Orsino and Olivia. He gives more details of Olivia's bereavement: her father died, leaving her in the care of her brother who died shortly after. Olivia's vow of seclusion is recounted again: 'she hath abjured the company/And sight of men'.

The Captain talks of Sebastian, Olivia and Orsino

The Captain is an excellent character witness. He gives testimony of the courage and determination of Sebastian when faced with imminent death in the shipwreck. He praises Olivia as a 'virtuous maid' and the Duke Orsino as a man of stature and nobility. Thus he encourages the audience to like these characters before they appear on stage.

Viola

Viola finds Orsino's bachelorhood of interest

Note that Viola already knew of Orsino, and she refers to the fact that 'he was a bachelor then'. The Captain confirms that this was still the case just a month before this shipwreck. Viola's awareness that the Duke is not married will shortly turn into something more.

Viola's almost melancholy wish that she might 'serve that lady' (Olivia) and perhaps participate in her sadness – as they both mourn brothers – until her own circumstances are improved, is quickly pushed aside. Viola is a positive character, in contrast to Olivia and Orsino (note how the latter waits until the very last Act before confronting Olivia herself with his love). She has a robust reaction to her loss, taking action to improve her situation: she will disguise herself as a man, seek employment, and hold on to the hope that her brother is still alive.

Appearance and reality

Disguise

Viola determines to seek employment in Orsino's household, disguised as a man. This is the first reference to the theme of disguise, or appearance and reality. It will be returned to on many other occasions as it is central to the action of the main plot, which turns on instances of mistaken identity.

Music

Note how Viola emphasises that music will help her gain entrance to the Duke's service: 'I can sing/And speak to him in many kinds of music'. This stresses the importance of music as a theme in the play: the play opened with music, and Orsino stressed its importance for love. This second scene ends with references to music, bringing the introduction of the main plot to an end. In the next scene the subplot is introduced.

In the first two scenes we are introduced to the main plot, which revolves around love and mistaken identity. We are also given brief details of the major characters involved in the main plot.

In Scene 2 the Captain, who appears to be a solid and unbiased witness, comments on various main characters:

Sebastian is 'provident in peril' and demonstrates 'courage and hope';

Orsino is 'A noble Duke, in nature as in name';

Olivia is 'fair' and 'a virtuous maid'.

Note how Viola's actions in Scene 2 show her to be very similar in character to her twin, Sebastian. By determining to seek employment, disguising herself as a man, and by her hopeful attitude towards her brother's survival, she also shows herself to be provident in peril, courageous and hopeful.

Act 1 Scene 3

After two very short scenes we are now introduced to the characters of the subplot: Sir Toby Belch, who is Olivia's uncle, Sir Andrew Aguecheek, an unwelcome suitor for Olivia, and Maria, Olivia's maid. The real purpose of encouraging Sir Andrew to pursue Olivia is so that Sir Toby may have him around as an accessible source of finance.

Harmony and disorder

Disorder

'I am sure care's an enemy to life' – Sir Toby suggests that his niece's vow is interfering with his own style of living, but equally it is relevant to how Olivia's vow is an 'enemy' to her own enjoyment of life – it takes the arrival of Cesario to change her attitude.

We have stepped 'downstairs' here. The poetry of the first two scenes, with references to love, music, passion, flowers and sorrow is replaced by much more down-to-earth style of conversation. Note how in the first two scenes the lines are in verse: here, the conversation is in prose, emphasising the contrast between the characters involved and their concerns.

Sir Toby is a drunkard who enjoys revelry. The disorder he creates is in marked contrast to the harmony sought by the main characters. We learn from Maria how Olivia is upset by Sir Toby's 'ill hours', i.e. his late-night drinking.

Sir Andrew Aguecheek

Sir Andrew Aguecheek

Maria reports Olivia's impressions of Sir Andrew Aguecheek – a 'foolish knight' – an accurate judgement. Note also Maria's assessment of him: 'fool', 'great quarreller' and 'coward'. Sir Toby's attitude to Sir Andrew is contemptuous: he openly makes fun of him, and shows how foolish he is. The description of him as a quarreller prepares us for when, later, he is persuaded to duel with Viola.

Sir Andrew's conversations with Maria and Sir Toby show him to be foolish and vain. He is easily persuaded to change his mind when he considers leaving for home and giving up his pursuit of Olivia.

Sir Toby Belch

It is obvious that Sir Toby does not really believe his niece will consider Sir Andrew as a prospective husband, and that he values Sir Andrew only for the money he can get from him for drink and as a butt for his humour. This throws light on the character of Sir Toby Belch – his surname is apt!

Scenes with Sir Toby and his friends are usually spoken in prose. Verse is reserved for the affairs of Olivia, Orsino, Viola and Sebastian.

Sir Toby Belch (his surname describes his character) is a drunkard who misuses his 'friend' Sir Andrew, spending his money and making jokes at his expense.

Sir Andrew is a foolish man, changeable and easily influenced.

We have now been introduced to three very different groups of characters, and the language each group uses is correspondingly different.

- At Orsino's court, the Duke speaks in verse and uses flowery, poetic imagery.

- The language spoken by Viola and the Captain is plainer as they are communicating and receiving information, but they speak verse because their conversation is important for the main plot.

- Sir Toby's language is full of robust vigour and energy. He is clearly intelligent and bandies words with Maria. His jokes are crude: 'Good Mistress Accost…"accost" is front her, board her, woo her, assail her.'

Act 1 Scene 4

In great contrast to the previous scene, this is the first love scene. Viola, now in the Duke's employ, using the name Cesario and disguised as a man, is to be sent to woo Olivia on Orsino's behalf. We learn that Orsino has quickly become very fond of 'Cesario' and that Viola has fallen in love with Orsino.

Love at first sight?

Love

The swiftness of Cesario's advancement, 'He hath known you but three days, and already you are no stranger' and her question, 'Is he (Orsino) inconstant, sir, in his favours?', suggest that already a bond is growing between the two, although there is as yet no indication that they are in love with one another. Of course, the fact that Viola is disguised as a man will put a barrier to such a relationship developing. Her question about Orsino's constancy perhaps shows she is already attracted to him and hopes his love for Olivia may not last.

Orsino tells us that he has told Cesario all the most private secrets of his soul – his faith and trust in her are remarkable considering their short acquaintance, but they lay the foundation for his sudden realisation later in the play that he loves her.

Ironically, Orsino refers to Cesario's youthful appearance and its resemblance to a maid: 'belie thy happy years/That say thou art a man'. This irony is further emphasised in Orsino's last lines of the scene, when he suggests Cesario might eventually 'call his (Orsino's) fortunes thine.'

Viola has a problem. She will carry out Orsino's instructions, but she has already decided that she would like to be his wife. Thus the first of the complicated love affairs is set in motion. Viola loves Orsino who, though attracted to her, is distracted from loving her because of her disguise as a man. However, Viola must disguise her love as she has the task of pleading his love for Olivia.

Act 1 Scene 5

We meet Feste and Malvolio for the first time, both in their professional roles: Feste as Olivia's jester, Malvolio as her steward. The first meeting between Cesario and Olivia takes place and, just as Viola fell in love with Orsino in the previous scene, so here Olivia falls in love with Cesario.

The initial part of the scene, involving Maria and Feste, provides light-hearted and witty conversation, in contrast to the intensity of Orsino telling of his love for Olivia in the previous scene.

Feste

Feste is an interesting character who moves freely between the various groupings: Orsino, Olivia and Sir Toby. However, he also keeps his distance – he is not really close to anyone in the play. Being a professional fool, with the task of being witty and amusing, is a precarious job. As a musician he also has a role to play in keeping that theme fresh in our minds; much of the music or praise of music in the play comes from him. He is a good judge of character, as will be seen. Here he helps lay the foundation for the audience's easy acceptance of Sir Toby's later marriage to Maria when he says: '...if Sir Toby would leave drinking, thou wert as witty a piece of Eve's flesh as any in Illyria.'

When Feste asks permission to prove that Olivia is a fool, he shows himself to be more clear-thinking than Olivia, pointing to the inconsistency of her mourning her dead brother for so long when she believes he is in heaven. His frankness is not welcomed by Malvolio, and their brief conversation gives Feste the opportunity to rebuke Malvolio sharply, repeating Sir Toby's opinion of Malvolio – he is a fool.

'Sick of self-love'

Olivia's comment to Malvolio that he is 'sick of self-love' is ironic. In a way, she suffers from the same fault: her mourning for her brother contains an element of self-pity. Her period of mourning actually lasts only a short time because she falls in love with Cesario. She is like Malvolio in another way too: she is proud, as Viola notes later in this scene.

Malvolio's position in Olivia's household seems assured, but it appears that he does not command her respect, nor that of anyone else. The ground is thus prepared for us to accept his downfall when it comes.

Viola determines to see Olivia

Malvolio's report of how Cesario had an answer for all his reasons as to why 'he' should not be admitted to see Olivia indicates 'his' quick wit and determination. This intrigues Olivia, who agrees to see Cesario.

Disguise

Olivia's decision to use a veil to 'disguise' her face is quickly replicated in effect by Cesario's ironic comment that 'I am not that I play'. The theme of disguise, for whatever reason, frequently occurs in the play. Olivia's comment that Cesario's words are 'like to be feigned' continues the theme. Note also how the references to 'sail', 'swabber' and 'hull' repeat the image of the sea and remind us of how Cesario came to be here, acting as Orsino's messenger. Cesario's comment, 'what I am and what I would are as secret as maidenhood', is an ironic reference to Viola's disguise.

Orsino

In a very generous speech, 'Your lord does know my mind… a gracious person…', Olivia praises Orsino: he is virtuous, noble, of great estate, learned, valiant, etc. Cesario's response is to tell Olivia how, were he in the Duke's place, he would be able neither to understand her rejection, nor accept it. Intrigued, she asks what he (Cesario) *would* do in that position.

'Make me a willow cabin'

Love

One of the most moving verses in the play, Cesario's words have great effect on Olivia and perhaps explain the interest she takes in Cesario. Certainly, Olivia's questions about Cesario's background and her willingness to see Cesario again, with the slight excuse of desiring to know how Orsino will take another rejection of his love, indicate a greater than normal interest in this messenger. This is confirmed immediately after Cesario's exit, when Olivia repeats some of the information she has gleaned about Cesario. Her words, 'I feel this youth's perfections...creep in at mine eyes', confirm the impact that Cesario has had.

'I do I know not what'

Olivia

The speed with which Olivia falls in love is matched by other incidents in the play. Viola already has affection for Orsino, as does he for 'Cesario': later, Sebastian will as quickly learn to love Olivia. But here, the impetuous nature of Olivia is seen when she sends Malvolio after Cesario with a ring which she says Cesario has left behind, and which she is determined that Cesario shall need to return. We ought to remember here Feste's comment that Olivia's long period of mourning for her brother made no sense. The truth of his words was obvious, and the swift development of Olivia's interest in Cesario makes us wonder how meaningful her mourning was.

The main plot – Olivia's love for Cesario and Viola's for Orsino – has been set in motion. The complications caused by Viola's disguise and her similarity to her brother Sebastian (yet to appear) have their origins here.

The subplot and its relationships are established. The theme of disguise (the difference between appearance and reality) will play a major part here, as in the main plot.

Note the contrast between the revelry and disorder of the subplot, and the romance of the main plot. This is reflected in the language used and in the style of conversation: verse for the main plot, prose for the subplot.

Feste acts as an almost independent figure. He demonstrates good judgement in his assessment of the various main characters. He provides much of the music in the play.

■ Self-test (Questions) Act One

Uncover the plot

Delete two of the three alternatives given, to find the correct plot. Beware possible misconceptions and muddles.

In Illyria/~~Elysium~~/~~Messina~~, the Duke ~~Carlo~~/Orsino/~~Cesario~~ is in love with ~~Olivia~~/Viola/~~Maria~~, who will see no-one, following the death of her ~~lover~~/father/~~brother~~. The shipwrecked ~~Olivia~~/Viola/~~Maria~~ disguises herself as a servant called ~~Fabian~~/~~Festa~~/Cesario: after only 3/~~6~~/~~7~~ days, 'he' is already the Duke's confidant, and is sent to woo Olivia/~~to sing to Olivia~~/~~to make his fortune~~. Olivia is attracted to 'the youth' – while 'he' already loves Valentine/~~Antonio~~/Orsino. Meanwhile, Sir Toby and Maria/~~Festa~~/~~Cujo~~ tease the foolish Sir Andrew ~~Agecloe~~/Aguecheek/~~Belch~~. Olivia is teased in turn by Sir Toby/Maria/Feste – to whom only the stuffy steward Valentine/Fabian/Malvolio takes exception.

What? Why? How? Where? When?

1 What is 'to season/A brother's dead love'?
2 What does Olivia say will take the sting out of a fool's insults?
3 What says Quinapalus?
4 Why does Orsino think Cesario will have better luck with Olivia? *young*
5 Why does Olivia think Cesario's speech in praise of her beauty is likely to be 'feigned'? *poetical* *heaven but nature love the idea(?) unseen*
6 How does Feste prove Olivia a fool?
7 How does Orsino love Olivia, according to Cesario?
8 Where was the Captian born?
9 Where does Viola say her brother is – and what does this mean?
10 When was Sir Andrew planning to leave, for how long is he persuaded to stay – and why?

Who said that?

1 Who says: 'How will she love when the rich golden shaft/Hath kill'd the flock of all affection else'?
2 Who says: 'For I can sing/And speak to him in many sorts of music'?
3 Who says: 'I am sure care's an enemy to life'?
4 Who says: 'I marvel your ladyship takes delight in such a barren rascal.'?
5 Who says: O, you are sick of selflove, Malvolio, and taste with a distemper'd appetite.'?

Open quotes

Find the line – and complete the phrase or sentence.
1 'If music be the food of love…'
2 'I have unclasp'd /To thee…'
3 'Yet, a barful strife!…'
4 'Yet I suppose him virtuous…'
5 'Make me a willow cabin at your gate…'

Let's talk about you

Who is describing whom in the following character portraits?
1 'A noble duke, in nature as in name'
2 'A virtuous maid, the daughter of a count'
3 'Hast a mind that suits/With this thy fair and outward character'
4 'Provident in peril'
5 'Besides that he's a fool, he's a great quarreller'
6 'As witty a piece of flesh as any in Illyria'
7 'He is very wellfavour'd and he speaks very shrewishly'

Virtual reality?

1 How does the Captain fulfil Viola's request: 'I prithee….Conceal me what I am'?
2 What remark of Viola's shows that she is cautious about judging by outward appearance?
3 Who has a 'secret soul' and to whom has he revealed it?
4 Who says: 'Wherefore are these things hid?' – to whom, and in what context?
5 Who says: 'I am not that I play', and what are the surface – and underlying – meanings of the phrase?
6 What is 'as secret as maidenhead'?
7 Whose face is hidden, and what image is used to describe the unveiling of it?
8 Quote the sentence in which 'invisible', 'subtle stealth' and 'creep' appear together.

Self-test (Answers) Act One

Uncover the plot

In Illyria, the Duke Orsino is in love with Olivia, who will see no-one, following the death of her brother. The shipwrecked Viola disguises herself as a servant called Cesario: after only 3 days, 'he' is already the Duke's confidant, and is sent to woo Olivia. Olivia is attracted to 'the youth' – while 'he' already loves Orsino. Meanwhile, Sir Toby and Maria lease the foolish Sir Andrew Aguecheek. Olivia is teased in turn by Feste – to whom only the stuffy steward Malvolio takes exception.

What? Why? How? Where? When?

1 Olivia's intended seven years veiled and in seclusion, and daily tears in her chamber 1,1
2 To be 'generous, guiltless and of free disposition' 1,5
3 'Better a witty fool than a foolish wit' 1,5
4 Because the show of passion will be more appealing in a younger 'man' 1,4
5 Because it is 'poetical' 1,5
6 By getting her to say that she mourns her brother even though she believes him to be in heaven 1,5
7 'With adorations, fertile tears, with groans that thunder love, with sighs of fire.' 1,5
8 In Illyria, three hours' journey from the shore where we meet him talking to Viola 1,2
9 In Elysium: dead (in paradise) 1,2
10 The following day; another month; because Sir Toby is living off his money 1,3

Who said that?

1 Orsino 1,1
2 Viola 1,2
3 Sir Toby Belch 1,3
4 Malvolio 1,5
5 Olivia 1,5

Open quotes

1 'If music be the food of love, play on:/Give me excess of it, that, surfeiting,/The appetite may sicken and so die.' 1,1
2 'I have unclasp'd /To thee the book even of my secret soul' 1,4
3 'Yet, a barful strife! /Whoe'er I woo, myself would be his wife.' 1,4
4 'Yet I suppose him virtuous, know him noble,/Of great estate, of fresh and stainless youth.' 1,5
5 'Make me a willow cabin at your gate/And call upon my soul within the house.' 1,5

Let's talk about you

1 Captain, of Orsino 1,1
2 Captain, of Olivia 1,1
3 Viola, of Captain 1,1
4 Captain, of Sebastian 1,1
5 Maria, of Sir Andrew 1,3
6 Feste, of Maria 1,5
7 Malvolio, of Cesario 1,5

Virtual reality?

1 By giving her man's clothes and recommending her to the Duke as a boy servant 1,2
2 'though that nature with a beauteous wall/Doth oft close in pollution.' 1,2
3 Orsino, to Cesario 1,4
4 Sir Toby to Sir Andrew – teasing him about hiding his 'gifts' and 'virtue' (for dancing) 1,3
5 Cesario/Viola. Surface: a comeback to Olivia's jibe about being a 'comedian'/actor. Underlying: we know that the boy Cesario is the woman Viola in disguise 1,5
6 What/who Cesario is, and what 'he' wants ('would') 1,5
7 Olivia's. Drawing the curtain away from in front of a painted portrait 1,5
8 'Methinks I feel this youth's perfections/With an invisible and subtle stealth/To creep in at mine eyes.' 1,5

Act 2 Scene 1

Sebastian, Viola's identical twin, is rescued from the sea by Antonio, a ship's captain. The similarity between Sebastian and Viola is stressed and the potential for mistaken identity underlined. Sebastian decides to go to Orsino's court.

Reminders of Act 1 Scene 1

Viola

This scene echoes Act 1 Sc 1: we are told who Sebastian is, his relationship to Viola, that they are twins and very similar in looks, that Viola is beautiful and intelligent ('she bore a mind that envy could not but call fair'), and that Sebastian has been shipwrecked on the same shore as Viola. Like Viola, he determines to go to Orsino's court.

Love and friendship

The relationship between Sebastian and Antonio reminds us of that between Viola and the Captain, although this relationship is clearly deeper because Antonio is willing to put himself in danger for Sebastian. Antonio's decision to follow Sebastian in

Sebastian

spite of danger to himself is important, as he will contribute to the confusions which arise from the similarity between Sebastian and Viola.

Like his sister, Sebastian is obviously liked by his companions and is generous in spirit. He has inspired so much affection in Antonio that the latter is willing to follow him anywhere: 'I do adore thee so,/That danger shall seem sport'.

Act 2 Scene 2

Olivia sends Malvolio to give her ring to Cesario, who realises Olivia has fallen in love with 'him'. She comments on the tangles of love and realises that time alone can sort out the confusion.

Malvolio delivers a message

Malvolio

Malvolio is obviously unhappy at having to pursue Olivia with the ring, but he reports Olivia's message accurately. However, his rudeness to Cesario, who has done him no harm, and his boorish act of throwing the ring to the ground help to prejudice the audience against him so that when he suffers, later in the play, there is not much sympathy for him.

Olivia declares her love for Cesario

Viola recognises that Olivia has been fooled by her disguise and of that disguise she says: 'I see thou art a wickedness,/Wherein the pregnant enemy does much'.

Disguise

She can sympathise with Olivia as she herself has the same problem with Orsino: 'and I...fond as much on him...My state is desperate for my master's love'. At the end of Act 1 Sc 2, Viola decided to leave the future for 'time' to sort out. Here she again decides that 'time, thou must untangle this, not I'. Time will indeed lead to the unravelling of the 'wickedness' that arises from disguise. That there is much to sort out is clear – Viola loves Orsino, who loves Olivia, who loves Cesario (Viola in disguise).

By the end of Act 2 Sc 2, all the elements of the main plot are in place:

- Viola, disguised as a man (Cesario), has quickly grown close to Orsino.
- Her duty is to plead Orsino's love to Olivia.
- Olivia has fallen in love with Cesario; Viola is in love with Orsino.
- Orsino is developing an affection for Cesario.
- Sebastian, Viola's identical twin, has survived the shipwreck and is making for Orsino's court.

Act 2 Scene 3

The drunken revelry of Sir Toby and friends is interrupted by Maria, who tries to quieten them. Malvolio arrives with the same intention and includes Maria in his criticism. Maria proposes they revenge themselves by writing him a letter in handwriting similar to Olivia's, suggesting Olivia is in love with him. As a result, they hope he looks a fool in front of Olivia.

Sir Toby indulges himself and Feste sings of love

Those excesses which Sir Toby demonstrated in Act 1 Sc 3 are again shown here. His determination to eat, drink and enjoy himself confirms him as a lover of the

Love

Music

good life. The extravagant, nonsense words of Sir Andrew – Pigrogromitus, Vapians, etc. underline the foolishness of the man's character.

Feste takes part in this scene, but he is not really one of them – it has already been noted that he moves easily between the major groups of characters. Here, his songs touch on the heart of the play: 'your true love's coming', and suggest that in the end all will be well: 'Journeys end in lovers meeting'. He also reminds us of Viola's comment that time will have to sort matters out: 'What's to come is still unsure'. Previously, Feste made some apt comments on Olivia's attitude to mourning: here he comments effectively on the development of the play and its central theme, love.

Feste is the character who is most strongly linked to the theme of music and here we see how music, whilst contributing to the overall atmosphere of the scene, is also used to support the words and actions of other characters.

Malvolio confronts Sir Toby

Disorder

Malvolio

Because he is a killjoy, Malvolio does not attract the audience's sympathy here, and so the plot against him is seen as a fair return. The fact that he is a Puritan also colours his view of Sir Toby's lifestyle. However, we should remember that he is Olivia's steward and it is his job to preserve her from Sir Toby's disorderly and disruptive behaviour.

Olivia dislikes Sir Toby's revelry and Maria suggests that he is in danger of being turned 'out of doors' for his noise. When Malvolio picks up this theme, it is not clear how far he is speaking for Olivia when he threatens that she is 'very willing to bid you farewell'.

Sir Toby's reminder to Malvolio that he is just a steward picks up his earlier comment to Maria, when he reminded her that he was 'consanguineous' (related by blood) to Olivia. He feels he has a special place in the household and that his position is unassailable. His rebuke to Malvolio, 'Dost thou think, because thou art virtuous, there shall be no cakes and ale?' highlights the contrast between fun-loving Sir Toby and strait-laced Malvolio.

It is typical of Sir Andrew that he suggests challenging Malvolio to a duel *after* Malvolio has left the scene. It also foreshadows the time, later in the play, when he will be persuaded to duel with Cesario.

Maria outlines the plot against Malvolio

Maria's counsel to Sir Toby to desist from his revelry for the time being is sensible. She tells how Olivia is unhappy and distracted since Cesario visited her. However, her plan to hoax Malvolio is effective in gaining Sir Toby's quiet attention.

Maria's plan hinges on her ability to disguise her handwriting to appear like Olivia's and on Malvolio's foolish ambition to become Olivia's husband. She will suggest that Olivia loves Malvolio and would like to see him dressed in a way that, in reality, Olivia hates. She will drop the letter where Malvolio will surely find it, and Sir Toby and friends can enjoy the scene from safe hiding places.

Sir Toby Belch

The plan having been laid and left in Maria's hands, she departs. The audience now gains new insight into Sir Toby's character. When Sir Andrew praises Maria, Sir Toby comments that she 'adores me'. However, his next words: 'what o'that?' are ungracious and selfish. They do not make him popular with the audience and tend to lessen any respect or liking we may have had for him. The words also confirm Feste's accurate assessment in Act 1 Scene 5 when he suggested that if Sir Toby could get his senses together he would recognise her talents. The other matter here is his quite open demand that Sir Andrew must obtain more money. His promise that Sir Andrew will marry Olivia in the end must fall rather flat on the audience's ears – he is obviously interested only in spending the money himself.

Sir Andrew's part in all this is very foolish: he takes part in the plot against Malvolio to see him humiliated before Olivia and blindly agrees to Sir Toby's demands for his money in the vain hope that he can buy Olivia's favour.

> **The subplot** against Malvolio has been prepared. He is to be deceived into thinking Olivia loves him. Maria will forge a letter in Olivia's handwriting and leave it where he will find it.
>
> **Malvolio** is pompous, overbearing, full of self-love, opinionated, and a fool to himself in imagining Olivia could love him.

Act 2 Scene 4

Orsino tells Cesario of his love for Olivia and then sends Cesario to Olivia again, with another message. Cesario tells the Duke that 'he' has affection for a woman who strongly resembles the Duke.

Viola suggests she is in love

Love

Orsino

Music

The re-entry of Orsino with his call, again, for music, changes the tone from revelry to that of love. Orsino's words echo the opening lines of the play. He senses that Cesario is in love and is surprised when told the woman involved resembles him and is about his age – this is as far as Viola dare go in declaring her love for Orsino! His advice to her – to choose a younger woman, as a man should be older than the one he loves – is ironic. In reality, Viola *is* in love with a man older than herself: Orsino!

There is a seriousness about this scene, shown by the return to verse and the call for music. Our first impressions of Orsino are reinforced by the advice he gives to Cesario and his suggestion that women are like roses: their 'flower, being once displayed, doth fall that very hour' – another affected pose. Surely if that were the case, there would be no point in pursuing any woman, let alone Olivia. It reminds us of the question we asked about Orsino in the first scene: is he really in love, or just playing at being in love?

Unrequited love

Feste enters and is again asked to sing: his song speaks of the central theme of the play, love. It speaks of unrequited love (i.e. love that is given and not returned) which brings unhappiness to the giver. Orsino's love for Olivia is not returned, nor is Olivia's for Cesario, and nor is Viola's for Duke Orsino. In singing of love, note that Feste declines to be paid for the music – he sings for pleasure.

Orsino

Feste again shows his clear vision of the characters of those around him. His comments that the Duke's tailor should make him a doublet of 'changeable taffeta' and that the Duke's 'mind is a very opal' show that he views the Duke as a changeable man whose mind is easily swayed. The truth of this will be seen at the end of the play when Orsino suddenly switches his affection from Olivia to Viola, though to be fair by then he has spent much time in Viola's company and has always admired 'Cesario'.

Viola talks of her love

Viola

Viola poses the problem that she faces in her love for the Duke. His suggestion that women cannot love to the same degree or with the same passion as men ('no woman's heart/So big to hold so much, they lack retention') is patently wrong, given what we know of Viola. Viola's response is to defend the power of women's love, but she almost goes too far when she gives an example of woman's love: 'My father had a daughter loved a man – /As it might be perhaps, were I a woman'. However, when questioned about this 'sister', she is in difficult waters.

Disguise

Viola's suggestion that concealment of love feeds 'like a worm i'the bud' to some extent echoes her earlier image: 'Disguise I see thou art a wickedness/Wherein the pregnant enemy does much' (Act 2 Sc 2). Viola really loves the Duke, in contrast to his sentimental imagining of his love for Olivia.

The conclusion of this scene sees Cesario dispatched again to Olivia with a jewel to give her. This reminds us of how Olivia gave a ring to Cesario. Viola is at the mercy of the disguise she has taken upon herself and suffers as a result.

Act 2 Scene 5

Malvolio picks up a letter and decides Olivia has written it to him. The comedy in this scene comes from Malvolio's interpretation of the letter. The humour of this scene and the

Malvolio

intentional deception of Malvolio contrasts and links with the previous scene, where Viola's genuine love for Orsino is unrecognised by him, whilst Olivia rejects his love.

More on Malvolio's character

Fabian says that Malvolio is the reason that he (Fabian) is out of favour with Olivia, so he would 'exult' if Malvolio were made a fool of. Adding more information, Maria reports how Malvolio has been 'practising behaviour to his own shadow this half-hour', conjuring up a picture of Malvolio preening himself, his actions and movements, so that they will have the greatest effect on any future onlooker. These comments lessen the audience's sympathy for Malvolio and make him an object of laughter.

Malvolio talks to himself

It is plain that Maria has prepared Malvolio for the trick because, as he wanders the garden talking to himself and rehearsing gestures and movements, he reflects that Maria had told him Olivia admired him. He begins to convince himself that Olivia gives him more respect than she gives anyone else. Next he considers becoming 'Count Malvolio', swiftly reassuring himself that it is possible: 'the lady of the Strachy married the yeoman of the wardrobe.' He fantasises about acting the lord of the manor, being gracious yet firm, calling for Sir Toby and telling him to stop getting drunk, and referring to Sir Andrew as a foolish knight. All of this is overheard with amusement but growing annoyance by Sir Toby, and it ensures that the audience has little sympathy with Malvolio when the trick is played.

Reading the letter

Disorder

Malvolio 'recognises' the hand as Olivia's and goes on to suggest he recognises individual letters. The letters M, O, A, and I have no special significance except that they are readily recognisable as forming part of Malvolio's name: enough for him to interpret the letter as addressed to him.

The letter's instructions are intended to convince him it is genuine: they instruct him to behave much as he does at present ('Be opposite with a kinsman, surly with servants') and dress in a way that is sure to offend Olivia.

Malvolio is completely taken in, convinced that the letter is from Olivia to him, and he resolves to do all it commands. The scene is set for his downfall.

Sir Toby appreciates Maria

Sir Toby Belch

When Malvolio departs, the onlookers express their delight that plan has begun successfully. Sir Toby goes so far as to suggest that not only could he marry Maria for the ingenuity of her plan, he could also be her slave. This is a far cry from his last remark about Maria in Act 2 Sc 3, and is the third reference in the play to Sir Toby and Maria's possible marriage – the audience is well prepared for this event.

Maria confirms that Olivia will find Malvolio's behaviour unacceptable: she abhors the colour yellow, detests the fashion of cross-garters, and will find his ever-smiling face out of keeping with her melancholy mood.

Viola's love for Orsino is made clear, but because she loves him she will continue to court Olivia on his behalf.

Feste sings of unrequited love (love given but not returned).

The anonymous letter tricks Malvolio into thinking that Olivia loves him. He is to wear yellow cross-garters and smile continuously in her presence.

Self-test (Questions) Act Two

Uncover the plot

Delete two of the three alternatives given, to find the correct plot. Beware possible misconceptions and muddles.

Another shipwreck survivor – Roderigo/Sebastian/Cesario – mourns a lost brother/sister/father, and heads for Olivia's house/Messina/Orsino's court. Continuing the action of Act 1 Sc 3/4/5, Malvolio gives Viola the ring: she realises that Orsino/Antonio/Olivia loves her, she loves Orsino/Antonio/Cesario, and Orsino loves Cesario/Viola/Olivia! The Duke sends for Feste/Curio/Cesario for music, and argues that men's love is weaker/stronger/more fickle than women's. Meanwhile, the revellers are berated by Malvolio/Feste/Fabian for bear-baiting/fighting/singing. A plan of revenge is devised by Maria/Feste/Sir Toby, whose voice/hand/handwriting is like Olivia's, to make Malvolio think Olivia wants to turn him out/marry him/turn out Sir Toby. As the plan works, Toby admires Maria – echoed by Fabian/Feste/Sir Andrew.

Who? What? Why? How?

1 Who believes that all that look on him love him?
2 Who thinks life 'consists of eating and drinking'?
3 What 'gives a very echo to the seat/Where love is throned'?
4 What do journeys end in?
5 What three lines, said by Viola, sum up the love triangle?
6 What five things is Malvolio persuaded to do that will alienate him from Olivia?
7 What three things persuade Malvolio that Olivia loves him?
8 Why will Sebastian not let Antonio accompany him – and why is it truer than he knows?
9 Why did the song of the previous night relieve the Duke's passion much?
10 How has Malvolio been practising his behaviour?

Who said that?

1 Who modestly says: 'though it was said she much resembled me, (she) was yet of many accounted beautiful' – and who is 'she'?
2 Who says: 'But come what may, I do adore thee so/That danger shall seem sport, and I will go'?

3 Who says: 'Have you no wit, manners, nor honesty, but to gabble like tinkers at this time of night?'?
4 Who says: 'If ever thou shalt love,/In the sweet pangs of it remember me' and why is this ironical?
5 Who says: 'I could marry this wench for this device'?

Open quotes

Find the line – and complete the phrase or sentence.

1 'O Time, thou must untangle this, not I....'
2 'Present mirth hath present laughter....'
3 'Dost thou think, because thou art virtuous...'
4 'There is no woman's sides....'
5 'Some are born great...'

Parallel lines

Where do the following lines from Act 1 find an echo in Act 2?

1 'What else may hap, to time I will commit.'
2 'He left this ring behind him,/Would I or not.'
3 'There is a fair behaviour in thee, Captain.'
4 'My brother he is in Elysium./Perchance he is not drown'd?/ 'It is perchance yourself were saved.'

Subtle hints

Find three speeches where Viola declares her love for Orsino – although only she and the audience know it!

Virtual reality?

1 Who is Roderigo – and what does this imply?
2 'If it be so – as 'tis' – then what, and why?
3 What is 'disguise', according to Viola?
4 What is 'like a worm i'th'bud'?
5 Who is The Fortunate Unhappy (in a sense, three different people)?
6 What three terms are used to describe Maria's use of M, O, A, I in the letter to Malvolio?

Self-test (Answers) Act Two

Uncover the plot

Another shipwreck survivor – Sebastian – mourns a lost sister, and heads for Orsino's court. Continuing the action of Act 1 Sc.5, Malvolio gives Viola the ring: she realises that Olivia loves her, she loves Orsino, and Orsino loves Olivia! The Duke sends for Feste for music, and argues that men's love is stronger than women's. Meanwhile, the revellers are berated by Malvolio for singing. A plan of revenge is devised by Maria, whose handwriting is like Olivia's, to make Malvolio think Olivia wants to marry him. As the plan works, Toby admires Maria – echoed by Sir Andrew.

Who? What? Why? How?

1 Malvolio 2,3
2 Sir Toby 2,3
3 The melody Viola and the Duke are listening to 2,4
4 Lovers meeting 2,3
5 'My master loves her dearly,/And I, poor monster, fond as much on him;/ And she, mistaken, seems to dote on me.' 2,2
6 Be confident of her love; be rude to others; wear yellow; be cross-gartered; smile continually 2,5
7 Maria has told him so; she treats him with respect; the letter forged by Maria 2,5
8 In case Sebastian's bad luck rubs off on Antonio: Antonio will be in danger at Orsino's court 2,1
9 Because it was old-fashioned, plain and innocent – not like the more modern songs 2,4
10 In the sunlight, talking to his shadow 2,5

Who said that?

1 Sebastian, of his sister (whom we suspect to be Viola) 2,1
2 Antonio 2,1
3 Malvolio 2,3
4 Orsino, because Viola is suffering the pangs of love for Orsino 2,4
5 Sir Toby 2,5

Open quotes

1 'O Time, thou must untangle this, not I.../It is too hard a knot for me t'untie!' 2,2
2 'Present mirth hath present laughter.../What's to come is still unsure.' 2,3
3 'Dost thou think, because thou art virtuous, there shall be no more cakes and ale?' 2,3
4 'There is no woman's sides can bide the beating of so strong a passion/As love doth give my heart.' 2,4
5 'Some are born great, some achieve greatness, and some have greatness thrust upon 'em.' 2,5

Parallel lines

1 'O time, thou must untangle this, not I.' 2,2
2 'Give her this jewel; say /My love can give no place, bide no delay.' 2,4
3 'I perceive in you so excellent a touch of modesty...' 2,1
4 'Some hour before you took me from the breach of the sea was my sister drown'd.' 2,1

Subtle hints

1 Viola says she is in love with someone of Orsino's complexion and years 2,4
2 'Say that some lady, as perhaps there is,/Hath for your love as great a pang of heart/As you have for Olivia.' 2,4
3 'My father had a daughter lov'd a man,/As it might be, perhaps, were I a woman,/I should love your lordship.' 2,4

Virtual reality?

1 Sebastian: he has concealed his name, even to his rescuer 2,1
2 Then Olivia 'were better love a dream' – because 'Cesario' isn't real 2,2
3 'A wickedness/Wherein the pregnant enemy does much.' 2,2
4 The concealment of love (by Cesario's supposed sister) eating away at her looks 2,4
5 The supposed writer of the letter penned by Maria: Malvolio is led to assume it is Olivia 2,5
6 A 'riddle', a 'dish o' poison' and a 'simulation' 2,5

Act 3 Scene 1

Cesario carries the Duke's message of love to Olivia once again, but this time Olivia openly speaks of her love for Cesario. Note that Viola changes from speaking prose to Feste, to speaking in verse when she addresses Olivia.

Cesario – 'a rare courtier'

Feste

Cesario and Feste indulge in some witty conversation and wordplay. Feste is respectful towards Cesario, but his remark about Cesario's need to grow a beard reminds Viola of her love for Orsino: she desperately *wants* a beard, but it belongs to Orsino; she does not want to grow one herself! When Feste leaves her, Viola muses on the difficult art of being a fool: 'a practice/As full of labour as a wise man's art'.

A brief conversation between Cesario, Sir Toby and Sir Andrew ensues. Sir Andrew is impressed by Cesario's vocabulary and refers to 'him' as a 'rare courtier'.

Olivia speaks out

After some verbal sparring, during which Olivia cannot quite bring herself to speak her heart, she finally declares her love for Cesario:

Disguise

> 'Cesario, by the roses of the spring,
> By maidhood, honour, truth, and everything,
> I love thee so, that, maugre all thy pride,
> Nor wit nor reason can my passion hide.'
>
> 3, 1

Cesario's reply gives Olivia hope: no woman has or ever will be mistress of 'his' heart. As a woman, Viola knows this to be true. Her disguise protects her against violent attack, but creates emotional confusion for herself and those around her.

Act 3 Scene 2

Sir Andrew, imagining Cesario to be a rival for Olivia's hand, is jealous of him. Sir Toby has no difficulty in persuading him to challenge Cesario to a duel. As a result of the challenge, events are set in motion which will move the various plots along, bringing Sebastian into the action. Maria reports that Malvolio is following the letter's instructions.

Sir Andrew is jealous of Cesario

Sir Andrew Aguecheck

Sir Andrew complains that Olivia is favouring Cesario far more than she ever did him. Fabian suggests that Olivia is doing this on purpose to make Sir Andrew jealous and to fire up his passion. Sir Toby persuades Sir Andrew that if he challenges Cesario to a duel and wins, Olivia will be impressed with his valour.

When Sir Andrew has left, Sir Toby says he will deliver Sir Andrew's challenge but does not think Sir Andrew and Cesario will actually fight. He has a low opinion of Sir Andrew's valour: he has 'so much blood in his liver as will clog the foot of a flea'.

Maria arrives to confirm that Malvolio is following the letter's instructions and that they should witness the scene.

Disorder

This and other scenes dealing with the subplot are in prose. Verse is reserved for the noble scenes of love and harmony.

Act 3 Scene 3

Sebastian is reintroduced. His arrival means that the issue of mistaken identity will soon come to the fore, and that Sir Andrew will be in for a surprise when he challenges Cesario to a duel.

Antonio's love and friendship for Sebastian

The reappearance of Antonio and Sebastian signals the next stage in the main plot. Antonio's love for Sebastian is reinforced: he wishes to protect him but, because he is a 'wanted man' in Illyria, he has to lie low. However, he offers Sebastian his purse, and it speaks highly of Sebastian's character that Antonio is willing to risk so much for him.

Sebastian

Coming immediately after Sir Andrew's decision to fight Cesario, Sebastian's reappearance prepares the ground for the problems of mistaken identity which have consequences in both the main and the subplots.

Olivia declares her love for Cesario, who has given an answer that perhaps gives false hope to Olivia – no woman has ever been mistress of 'his' heart.

Sir Andrew is jealous of the attention Olivia gives to Cesario and, incited by Sir Toby, determines to challenge 'him' to a duel.

Sebastian, Viola's twin, and his friend Antonio arrive in the city where they part company for a while.

Act 3 Scene 4

Malvolio enters, dressed in the manner suggested in the letter written by Maria – the letter he thinks Olivia wrote to him. Olivia, finding his behaviour very strange, commits him to the care of her servants. Cesario is challenged to a duel by Sir Andrew, but is rescued by Antonio. When Antonio addresses her as 'Sebastian', she is given hope that her brother might still be alive.

Olivia is in love

Olivia's first words show that she is very much in love with Cesario: 'How shall I feast him? What bestow of him?' To calm herself down, she calls for her 'sad and civil' servant Malvolio.

'Some have greatness thrust upon them'

Disguise

But when Malvolio arrives, he is very changed: smiling and cross-gartered, he attempts to engage Olivia in witty conversation. Olivia's suggestion that he should go to bed he takes to be an invitation to *her* bed. He knowingly quotes 'Olivia's' letter to her: her response is that he suffers from 'midsummer madness'. News of Cesario's arrival distracts her attention and she instructs Maria to place Malvolio in her servants' care.

Malvolio thinks Olivia's behaviour complies exactly with 'her' letter. His reason is blunted by his own fevered imaginings of his coming greatness.

Disorder

Sir Toby, Maria and Fabian enjoy themselves hugely at Malvolio's expense. Sir Toby thinks his wits are affected: 'His very genius hath taken the infection of the device'. Fabian agrees: 'we shall make him mad indeed'. Sir Toby proposes binding Malvolio and putting him into a dark room as though he *were* a madman: more fun at Malvolio's expense.

Sir Andrew's challenge and Sir Toby's pleasure

Sir Toby Belch

Sir Andrew's challenge shows his foolishness: it makes little sense and will only confuse Cesario. Having encouraged Sir Andrew to his face, Sir Toby gives his real judgement on the letter once he has gone; it is 'excellently ignorant'. Praising Cesario's 'good capacity and breeding', Sir Toby says he will not deliver Sir Andrew's letter, because it will 'breed no terror' in Cesario. He determines to deliver the challenge by word of mouth. Note how he takes little account of the feelings of either Cesario or Sir Andrew – his only consideration is his own enjoyment.

The duel is important because it causes Antonio to mistake Viola for Sebastian and gives Viola hope that her brother might be alive.

Cesario resists Olivia's pleading

Viola

Meanwhile Olivia has been declaring her love to Cesario, but has received no encouragement: 'I have said too much unto a heart of stone'. Viola demonstrates great loyalty to Orsino, in spite of her love for him and in the face of Olivia's declarations of love. It would perhaps have been easier for her to undermine Orsino's quest for Olivia's hand in order to improve her own chances with Orsino. But her integrity is such that she does the job Orsino has given her.

The duel

Sir Toby accosts Cesario, warning that Sir Andrew intends to challenge 'him' to a duel. He declares that Sir Andrew has already killed three men: 'Souls and bodies hath he divorced three'. Cesario is, reluctant ('A little thing would make me tell them how much I lack of a man') but, at Sir Toby's insistence, draws her sword.

Disguise

When Cesario and Sir Andrew meet, the comedy of the situation lies in their mutual fear, which is understandable, given Sir Toby's efforts to disguise the reality of the situation from them both. This is another example of disguise confusing appearance and reality during the course of this long scene.

Viola is given hope that her brother lives

Hardly have swords been drawn when Antonio appears and, mistaking her for Sebastian, declares he will fight on Cesario's behalf. This is prevented by the arrival of officers of the peace, who arrest Antonio 'at the suit of Count Orsino'.

Viola

Disguise

Antonio, bound for prison, asks Cesario for his (Antonio's) purse. Although confused, Viola volunteers to lend him half her money, regardless of their short acquaintance – another pointer to her generous character. Antonio is astounded, and the more he protests against 'Sebastian's' rejection of their friendship, the more puzzled Cesario becomes.

When Antonio describes how he snatched his friend from the jaws of death, and addresses him as 'Sebastian', the first step is taken towards the unravelling of the misunderstandings caused by Viola's disguise. The fact that Antonio could mistake Viola for her brother Sebastian also lends credibility to the mistake that Olivia will shortly make in believing that Sebastian is Cesario.

The departure of Antonio with the officers leaves Viola to wonder and hope. Denied the opportunity to question Antonio further, she can but hope 'Prove true, imagination, O prove true – ...O, if it prove/Tempests are kind, and salt waves fresh in love!'

Malvolio delights Sir Toby and his friends by following all the letter's instructions. Wearing yellow stockings and crossgarters, and smiling continuously, he appears ridiculous, and Olivia thinks he has lost his wits. As a result he will find himself treated like a real madman, and at Sir Toby's mercy.

Cesario rejects Olivia's declarations of love, but continues to court her on Orsino's behalf.

The duel between Sir Andrew and Cesario is interrupted when Antonio intervenes, but he is then arrested. The fact that he has mistaken her for her brother gives Viola hope that Sebastian may be alive.

Self-test (Questions) Act Three

Uncover the plot

Delete two of the three alternatives given, to find the correct plot. Beware possible misconceptions and muddles.

Following orders from Act 2 Sc 2/3/4, Cesario comes to return Olivia's ring/press the Duke's suit/declare his love. Olivia declares her love for Orsino/Malvolio/Cesario. Sir Toby/Sir Andrew/Fabian is jealous and, egged on, writes a sonnet/licence/challenge. Meanwhile Sebastian arrives with Antonio/Valentine/the Captain, who lends him his ring/purse/dagger so that he can see the town/find lodgings/find food. Curio/Feste/Malvolio plays the fool – depressed only because Olivia doesn't respond/Sir Toby teases him/cross-gartering cuts off his circulation! Ignoring Sir Andrew's/Orsino's/Maria's letter, Sir Toby conveys challenges, telling each party that the other is a coward/devil/knight. They are parted by Antonio/Sebastian/the Captain, who is arrested and, asking for his sword/purse/sea-cap, accuses Viola/Sir Toby/Olivia of ingratitude: Viola realises he mistakes her for Cesario/Orsino/Sebastian.

Who? What? Why? How?

1 Who is 'sad and civil' – and why is the comment ironic?
2 Who is 'a very devil' and who is 'quick, skilful and deadly' – according to whom, and why?
3 What was Antonio's crime against Orsino?
4 What confirms Malvolio in his belief in the letter's truthfulness?
5 What is 'more matter for a May morning' – and what was the previous 'matter'?
6 What first gives Viola hope that Sebastian is alive?
7 What evidence of cowardice do Sir Toby and Fabian use to make Sir Andrew pursue the duel?
8 Why, according to Fabian, has Olivia shown favour to Cesario?
9 Why is Viola willing to give money to Antonio – and why does he expect it?
10 How does Sir Toby respond when Fabian remarks how 'dear' Sir Andrew has been to him?

Who said that?

1 Who says: 'I love thee so that, maugre all thy pride,/Nor wit nor reason can my passion hide'?
2 Who says: 'My willing love/The rather by these arguments of fear./Set forth in your pursuit'?
3 Who says: O, if it prove,/Tempests are kind, and salt waves fresh in love'?
4 Who says: 'I have said too much unto a heart of stone'?
5 Who says: 'You are idle shallow things; I am not of your element'?

Open quotes

Find the line – and complete the phrase or sentence.
1 'This fellow is wise enough to play the fool;....'
2 'I have one heart...'
3 'If this were played upon a stage now,....'
4 'None can be call'd deform'd....'
5 'Prove true, imagination, O, prove true....'

Parallel lines

Where do the following lines from Acts 1 and 2 find an echo in Act 3?
1 'You waste the treasure of your time.' 'In delay there lies no plenty'
2 'I am not that I play'
3 'I have many enemies in Orsino's court'
4 'Who I am and what I would are as secret as maidenhead'
5 'Give her this jewel'; 'We will draw the curtain and show you the picture'

Virtual reality?

1 Identify three reminders that Cesario is not a man.
2 How do we first realise that Antonio takes Viola/Cesario for Sebastian, and what words of Viola's therefore cause anger and confusion?
3 Who claims mistaken identity – but is not believed?
4 Who is a self-confessed 'corrupter of words', and what words does he use to show how deceptive words can be?
5 What does 'as horribly conceited of him' mean, and why is this relevant to the theme of 'deception'?
6 How does Viola admit that she has been imitating in her disguise?

Self-test (Answers) Act Three

Uncover the plot

Following orders from Act 2 Sc. 4, Cesario comes to press the Duke's suit. Olivia declares her love for Cesario. Sir Andrew is jealous, and, egged on, writes a challenge. Meanwhile Sebastian arrives with Antonio, who lends him his purse so that he can see the town. Malvolio plays the fool – depressed only because cross-gartering cuts off his circulation! Ignoring Sir Andrew's letter, Sir Toby conveys challenges, telling each party that the other is a devil. They are parted by Antonio, who is arrested and, asking for his purse, accuses Viola of ingratitude. Viola realises he mistakes her for Sebastian.

Who? What? Why? How?

1 Malvolio – because he is just about to show himself anything but! 3,4
2 Cesario and Sir Andrew – according to Sir Toby; to make them terrified to fight each other 3,4
3 Refusing to return what was taken in the sea fight against the Duke's galleys 3,3
4 Olivia sends Sir Toby to attend him; the letter has told him to 'appear stubborn to him' 3,4
5 The joke of Sir Andrew's challenge to Cesario: Malvolio's apparent madness before Olivia 3,4
6 Antonio reproaches her by the name of Sebastian, for ingratitude 3,4
7 Viola's apparent failure to stand by her supposed friend, Antonio 3,4
8 In order to make Sir Andrew jealous 3,2
9 His help (with the duel) and his predicament. He thinks she is Sebastian, to whom he has lent it 3,4
10 That in fact it is he who has been 'dear' (expensive) to Sir Andrew – by getting money from him 3,2

Who said that?

1 Olivia 3,1
2 Antonio 3,3
3 Viola 3,4
4 Olivia 3,4
5 Malvolio 3,4

Open quotes

1 This fellow is wise enough to play the fool; And to do that well craves a kind of wit.' 3,1
2 'I have one heart, one bosom and one truth,/And that no woman has.' 3,1
3 'If this were played upon a stage now, I would condemn it as an improbable fiction.' 3,4
4 'None can be call'd deform'd but the unkind./Virtue is beauty.' 3,4
5 'Prove true, imagination, O, prove true,/That I, dear brother, be now ta'en for you!' 3,4

Parallel lines

1 'The clock upbraids me with the waste of time' 3,1
2 'I am not what I am.' 3,1
3 'I do not without danger walk these streets.' 3,3
4 'Who you are and what you would are out of my welkin.' 3,1
5 'Here, wear this jewel for me – it is my picture.' 3,4

Virtual reality?

1 'I am almost sick for one (a beard); though I would not have it grow on my chin.' 3,1
2 'I have one heart, one bosom, and one truth, And that no woman has' 3,1
3 'A little thing would make me tell them how much I lack of a man.' 3,4
4 Antonio challenges Sir Andrew 'for his love.' Viola says 'what money, sir?' and then denies she knows him 3,4
5 Antonio: 'You do mistake me, sir.' It doesn't work: 'he knows I know him well.' 3,4
4 Feste. He compares a sentence to a kid glove: 'How quickly the wrong side may be turn'd outward.' He also calls words 'wanton', 'rascals' and 'false' 3,1
5 Imagines/wrongly believes the same horrible things about him: the blood-thirsty opponents 'feared by Sir Andrew and Cesario are only phantoms created by Sir Toby and Fabian. 3,4
6 Her twin, Sebastian 3,4

Act 4 Scene 1

Mistaking Sebastian for Cesario and attacking him, Sir Andrew is very surprised when he to finds himself being beaten. Sir Toby intervenes and draws his sword against Sebastian, but when Olivia enters and discovers Sir Toby duelling, she banishes him from her sight. Sebastian meets Olivia for the first time and is instantly attracted to her—she, of course, thinks he is Cesario.

Sir Andrew strikes Sebastian – mistaken identities abound

The next stage in the discovery of Sebastian and the playing out of his part in the main plot now takes place. Sent by Olivia to bring Cesario to her, Feste has chanced upon Sebastian whom he mistakes for Cesario. Sebastian, much to Feste's surprise, denies that he is called Cesario or that he knows Feste's lady.

Disguise

In the midst of their dispute they meet Sir Andrew and Sir Toby. Sir Andrew takes Sebastian by surprise and strikes him, being under the impression that he is addressing Cesario: another case of mistaken identity. Sebastian gives Sir Andrew a beating with the handle of his dagger, at the same time exclaiming everyone he meets seems mad!

Love at first sight – Olivia's dreams come true?

The eruption of the fight between Sir Andrew and Sebastian into a serious affair involving Sir Toby is not allowed to develop. Olivia arrives and soundly berates and banishes Sir Toby, then turns her attention to Sebastian, whom she, too, mistakes for Cesario.

Disguise

She addresses him with affection and invites him into her house. Sebastian, though surprised and confused, is also delighted, and willingly agrees to be 'ruled' by her. His agreement is happily received by Olivia 'O, say so, and so be!' He cannot work out whether he is mad, or in an agreeable dream. Olivia's dreams also appear to have come true.

Act 4 Scene 2

The scene changes to the dark room where Malvolio has been imprisoned by Sir Toby and friends. Feste, disguised as Sir Topas the curate, discusses Malvolio's madness with him. Sir Toby, worried that he has seriously offended his niece, tells Feste to end the 'game'. Malvolio is given pen and paper to write to Olivia, explaining his behaviour.

Malvolio is confused – Sir Toby is worried

The continuation of the subplot against Malvolio interrupts the main plot, leaving the audience to wonder how Sebastian is going to react to Olivia, and whether she has actually gained her heart's desire.

Disguise

Malvolio has been imprisoned in a dark room. Maria persuades Feste to disguise himself as Sir Topas, the curate, and to visit Malvolio. Instead of helping Malvolio, he taunts and confuses him, telling him he is not in a dark room but in a house that is full of light, finally concluding that Malvolio is mad and shall remain there until he (Sir Topas) is convinced he is sane.

Sir Toby, however, is now afraid he might have gone too far and wishes for Malvolio to be released. He does not want to lose his position in Olivia's house. Malvolio at last prevails upon Feste to provide him with writing materials so that he can explain his behaviour to Olivia.

Act 4 Scene 3

Olivia persuades Sebastian that he should marry her at once, and fetches a priest to carry out the ceremony.

Olivia marries her 'Cesario'

Sebastian

Sebastian finds his situation almost unbelievable and has to convince himself that everything around him is real. He knows he is not mad and considers briefly whether Olivia is. However, he reasons that she would not be able to command such a large household if she were mad. His reasoning is sound, and he provides further comment on Olivia's intelligence and capabilities. One may wonder at Sebastian's behaviour. He is much more impulsive than his sister who, despite enormous temptation, has not declared her love for Orsino.

Olivia

Olivia brings a priest to carry out the marriage ceremony and Sebastian agrees to marry her. It is not surprising that, as Sebastian seems willing to accept her love, Olivia acts quickly to seal their marriage. Rejected for so long by Cesario and having had sufficient time to test her own feelings about 'him', she moves with decisiveness when the opportunity presents itself.

It is interesting to note that Olivia suggests the marriage should be kept secret until such time as Sebastian wishes it to be announced: more deception and disguise. Her motives for this are not clear: perhaps she feels that 'Cesario' might need time to explain 'his' action to 'his' master, Orsino. Whatever the reason, her action fits well with one of the major themes in the play.

> **Malvolio**, imprisoned as a madman, is interrogated by Feste, disguised as Sir Topas the curate – an already bemused Malvolio is even further confused.
>
> Though confused by the strength and suddenness of her affection, **Sebastian marries Olivia**.

Self-test (Questions) Act Four

Uncover the plot

Delete two of the three alternatives given, to find the correct plot. Beware possible misconceptions and muddles.

Feste, sent to find Orsino/Cesario/Olivia, finds Sebastian/Antonio/Viola instead. So does Sir Toby/Sir Andrew/Fabian, who follows up his final threat of Act 3 Sc 2/3/4 by striking 'Cesario': Sebastian hits back/draws his sword/throws his dagger. A real fight is prevented by Olivia/Viola/Antonio, who mistakes Sebastian for Orsino/Cesario/Sir Topas and is angry at Sir Andrew/Fabian/Sir Toby. Fabian/Feste/Maria dresses as Sir Toby/Sir Topas/Pythagoras, who confirms that Malvolio is mad – but Sir Toby is afraid/keen/embarrassed to carry the joke further. Meanwhile, Sebastian, amazed that Olivia/Maria/Viola loves him, agrees to marry her/live at peace with her/celebrate with her.

Who? What? Why? How?

1 Who is an 'ungracious wretch'/Fit for the mountains and the barbarous caves'?
2 Who does Sebastian wish to ask for advice – and why is this impossible?
3 Who is finally ready to fight Sebastian/Cesario for real?
4 What three things does Malvolio claim have been done to drive him mad?
5 What has Olivia given Sebastian – and what other occasions does this echo?
6 What does Malvolio ask Sir Topas for?
7 Why does Sir Toby decide to abandon his 'sport'?
8 Why are Sebastian and Sir Andrew both surprised by their encounter?
9 How does Olivia run her affairs?
10 How does Sebastian convince himself that neither he nor Olivia is mad?

Who said that?

1 Who says: 'I say there was never man thus abus'd'?
2 Who says: 'Then you are mad indeed, if you be no better in your wits than a fool.' – and to whom?
3 Who says: 'I'll...go with you./And, having sworn truth, ever will be true'?
4 Who says: 'Blame not this haste of mine' – and why is this particularly striking to Sebastian?
5 Who says: 'I would we were well rid of this knavery'?

Open quotes

Find the line – and complete the phrase or sentence.

1 'And hear thou there how many fruitless pranks... '
2 'If it be thus to dream,.... '
3 'I would I were the first... '
4 'Plight me the full assurance of your faith... '
5 'And though 'tis wonder that enwraps me thus... '

Virtual reality?

1 Why does Feste say: 'Nothing that is so is so' – and why is this ironic?
2 What does Sebastian first think when Olivia treats him like Cesario?
3 What disguise does Feste 'dissemble' in as Sir Topas, and why is this odd?
4 Who is told he 'counterfeits well' – and has the gall to ask Malvolio if he 'counterfeits' madness?
5 What concealment is Olivia willing to agree to?
6 Who suggests that who is mad in this Act?

Mistaken identity

Fill in the blanks suggested by the following deluded openings and bemused replies.

1 'Will you make me believe that I am not sent for you?'
   'I prithee vent thy folly somewhere else. Thou know'st not me. '
   ....is mistaken for........by.............
2 'Now, sir, have I met you again? There's for you.'
   'Why, there's for thee, and there, and there. Are all the people mad?'
   ....is mistaken for........by.............
3 'I prithee, gentle friend... '
   'What relish is in this? How runs the stream?'
   ....is mistaken for........by.............

Self-test (Answers) Act Four

Uncover the plot

Feste, sent to find Cesario, finds Sebastian instead. So does Sir Andrew, who follows up his final threat of Act 3 Sc 4 by striking 'Cesario': Sebastian hits back. A real fight is prevented by Olivia, who mistakes Sebastian for Cesario and is angry at Sir Andrew. Feste dresses as Sir Topas, who confirms that Malvolio is mad – but Sir Toby is afraid to carry the joke further. Meanwhile, Sebastian, amazed that Olivia loves him, agrees to marry her.

Who? What? Why? How?

1. Sir Toby 4,1
2. Antonio. He thinks he has just missed him – he is actually under arrest 4,3
3. Sir Toby 4,1
4. He has been locked up, kept in darkness, and sent a minister 4,2
5. A pearl: she has already sent Cesario a ring and given him a jewel/portrait 4,3
6. Pen, ink, paper and candle 4,2
7. Because it is dangerous: he is already in trouble with Olivia 4,2
8. Sir Andrew expects the 'cowardly' Cesario. Sebastian knows nothing of the previous quarrel 4,1
9. With a 'smooth, discreet and stable bearing' 4,3
10. Sebastian knows the air, sun and pearl for what they are. Olivia manages her household well 4,3

Who said that?

1. Malvolio 4,2
2. Sir Topas (Feste) to Malvolio 4,2
3. Sebastian 4,3
4. Olivia. It seems hasty to her, and she has 'courted' Cesario: as far as Sebastian is concerned, they have only just met 4,3
5. Sir Toby 4,2

Open quotes

1. 'And hear thou there how many fruitless pranks/This ruffian hath botched up' 4,1
2. 'If it be thus to dream, still let me sleep!' 4,1
3. 'I would I were the first that ever dissembled in such a gown.' 4,2
4. 'Plight me the full assurance of your faith/That my most jealous and too doubtful soul/May live at peace.' 4,3
5. 'And though 'tis wonder that enwraps me thus/Yet 'tis not madness' 4,3

Virtual reality?

1. Because Sebastian (whom he thinks is Cesario) denies that he knows him. Feste is only being sarcastic – but in fact he is quite right 4,1
2. 'Or (either) I am mad, or else this is a dream.' 4,1
3. A gown and beard. Because, as Sir Toby points out, Malvolio cannot see him anyway
4. The Clown 4,2
5. The concealment of her marriage to the supposed Cesario 4,3
6. Sebastian suggests that Feste is mad (4,1), that everybody is mad (4,1), that he himself is mad (4,1;4,3) and that Olivia is mad (4,3). Meanwhile, the Clown/Sir Topas calls Malvolio mad (4,2)

Mistaken identity

1. Sebastian is mistaken for Cesario by Feste 4,1
2. Sebastian is mistaken for Cesario by Sir Andrew and Sir Toby 4,1
3. Sebastian is mistaken for Cesario by Olivia 4,1

Act 5 Scene 1

The final Act resolves the various tangles of main plot and subplot. The Duke decides to court Olivia in person. Cesario is accused by Antonio of being 'ungrateful'; is accused by Olivia of breaking an appointment; is accused by Sir Andrew and Sir Toby of beating them and is accused by Orsino of failing to gain him Olivia's love. Sebastian's arrival unravels the misunderstandings. Malvolio's letter is read and the trickery of 'Olivia's' letter explained. Orsino declares his love for Viola and proposes marriage. The play ends with a song from Feste.

Orsino decides to confront Olivia

So far, Orsino's courtship of Olivia has been done through Cesario. Now he takes matters into his own hands. With all the main characters assembled, the misunderstandings can finally be resolved. Orsino's conversation with Feste lightheartedly underlines one of the themes of the play: deception.

Viola

Antonio enters under guard, and Cesario identifies him as the man who rescued 'him' from the duel. Orsino recognises him as a pirate who once attacked his fleet. Antonio complains of Cesario's ingratitude, of how Antonio rescued 'him' from the sea, risked arrest in order to accompany 'him', and even loaned 'him' his purse, only to be denied by 'that most ungrateful boy' when Antonio needed his help.

Cesario is as confused as the Duke by these allegations, and the Duke denies that they can be true, confirming that Cesario has been with *him* for the past three months. Further argument is prevented by Olivia's arrival.

Olivia is confounded

Orsino

Olivia again rejects Orsino's love and his response is angry, perhaps the first time he has spoken his mind. His vow to 'sacrifice' Cesario, whom he admits that he loves 'dearly', simply because he knows Olivia loves him, indicates the turmoil in his own heart. Viola now speaks out, declaring willingness to die 'a thousand deaths' for Orsino.

Olivia's clear rejection of Orsino releases Viola from her function as Orsino's agent. She can now declare that she loves him and is willing to follow him. This brings a horrified response from Olivia: 'Ay me, detested! How am I beguiled!' and she calls for the priest to back up her claim that she is Cesario's wife.

Disguise

Viola stands accused by all

When the priest confirms he has married Cesario and Olivia, Viola is trapped by her disguise. The Duke calls her a 'dissembling cub', whilst Olivia begs her to tell the 'truth'. Then Sir Andrew enters and recounts how his head has been broken and Sir Toby given a 'bloody coxcomb too' during the duel with 'Cesario'. Sir Toby and Feste confirm Sir Andrew's story: Viola stands accused on both sides.

Sebastian and Viola united – identities unmasked

Sebastian

When Sebastian enters, Orsino sums up the vision before them, and encapsulates the amazement of all: 'One face, one voice, one habit, and two persons!/A natural perspective, that is and is not.' Sebastian, unaware for the moment of the sensation he has created, makes haste to apologise to Olivia for injuring her uncle, Sir Toby. He greets Antonio with great affection.

His surprise is complete when he sees Cesario, exclaiming: 'I never had a brother...I had a sister whom the blind waves and surges have devoured'. Brother and sister 'test' each other about their father and childhood to make sure of each other's identity. Now Viola can tell the truth, at last, about herself. Orsino says that he too would like to share in this amazing revelation of Cesario being a woman. He wants to see her in her 'woman's weeds'.

Malvolio's letter – Orsino's proposal – Sir Toby and Maria are married

Feste delivers Malvolio's letter protesting his sanity, which convinces Olivia that he is not mad. She asks for him to be brought before her.

Happy at the way things have turned out, Orsino realises he is in love with Viola, having grown to love her while she was disguised as Cesario. He proposes marriage to her and, given Viola's love for him, we may assume she accepts.

Malvolio

Malvolio arrives and produces 'Olivia's' letter as evidence that she has 'misused' him. Olivia recognises Maria's handwriting and realises that he has been hoaxed. Fabian admits that what she says is true, but pleads that it should not spoil the happiness of the moment because, realising that his trick has put Maria in a difficult position, Sir Toby has married her.

Feste cannot resist goading Malvolio, misquoting his lines on greatness: 'and some have greatness *thrown* upon them' and revealing that *he* was 'Sir Topas'. He echoes Viola's belief that only time can sort matters out when he says 'the whirligig of time brings in his revenges'. But Malvolio refuses to be placated. Outraged that he has been made to look foolish, he leaves with threats to have revenge on everyone. Feste has the final word. Throughout the play, he has stood apart from the action and commented on it.

Orsino arrives to woo Olivia in person.

Viola is accused of disloyalty by Antonio, Orsino, and Olivia.

Sebastian and Viola are reunited and Viola reveals her true identity.

Orsino proposes to Viola and we learn that **Sir Toby** has married Maria.

Malvolio learns that he has been tricked, and vows to have revenge.

Self-test (Questions) Act Five

Uncover the plot

Delete two of the three alternatives given, to find the correct plot. Beware possible misconceptions and muddles.

Orsino/Viola/the Captain finally arrives at Olivia's house, in time to back up Viola/Malvolio/Sir Toby against the accusations of Sebastian/Olivia/Antonio. Olivia rejects Cesario's/Sebastian's/the Duke's love: enraged, he threatens Olivia/Cesario/Malvolio, but it is too late. The Captain/Sebastian/Valentine turns up and all becomes clear. Viola, united with the Duke/Antonio/the Captain, asks for Malvolio/Antonio/the Captain to be set free. Olivia, married to Cesario/Sebastian/Orsino, will be Orsino's lover/subject/sister. A letter from Fabian/Sir Toby/Malvolio gains his release. All is well, and the stage is left to Malvolio/Feste/the Duke.

Who? What? Why? Where? How?

1 Who is Antonio, depending on the point of view of three other characters?
2 Who will be both 'plaintiff' and 'judge' in the trial of the subplot conspirators?
3 What does Antonio say he has given Sebastian?
4 What is 'as fat and fulsome to mine ear/As howling after music' – and what was the music?
5 What has happened (all this time) to the Captain who rescued Viola?
6 What is Sebastian's assumption on seeing Viola? What is hers on seeing him?
7 Why has Sir Toby married Maria, according to Fabian?
8 Why does Fabian ask for leniency?
9 Where does Cesario go, when he is asked this question by Olivia?
10 How do Viola and Sebastian realise that they are brother and sister?

Who said that?

1 Who says: 'And I, most jocund, apt, and willingly,/To do you rest, an thousand deaths would die'?
2 Who says: 'Be that thou know'st thou art' – why, and why is this ironic?
3 Who says: 'How have the hours rack'd and tortur'd me/Since I have lost thee'?
4 Who says: 'If this be so, as yet the glass seems true,/I shall have share in this most happy wreck'?
5 Who says: 'I'll be reveng'd on the whole pack of you'?

Open quotes

Find the line – and complete the phrase or sentence.
1 'That very envy and the tongue...'
2 'I'll sacrifice the lamb that I do love...'
3 'One face, one voice...'
4 'You shall from this time be...'
5 'How with a sportful malice it was follow'd...'

About time

1 How long has the action of the play taken?
2 How long after Antonio lent his purse to Sebastian did he claim it back from Cesario?
3 How long have Sebastian and Olivia been married at the end of the play?
4 What 'brings in his revenges', according to Feste?
5 When what 'convents' (is convenient) will the Duke and Viola marry?

Knots and unravellings

With one exception, Viola is genuinely perplexed by the accusations made against her in this Act. Can you work it out? Fill in the blanks.

.... accuses Viola of .... because she denied him and his purse, when he thought she was .... She claims mistaken identity, backed up by .... – because he knows nothing of .... 's existence, and knows that .... has been with him for months.

.... accuses Viola of .... because she thinks she is .... , who has in fact missed their appointment: we find out why when .... and .... turn up and accuse Viola of .... (........ later apologises for this.)

.... accuses Viola (quite rightly, as it happens) of .... instead of wooing her on his behalf. With less justice, he then accuses her of .... because he thinks .... has married Olivia, a fact mistakenly affirmed by both .... and .... In fact, of course, it is .... who has married Olivia.

■ Self-test (Answers) Act Five

Uncover the plot

Orsino finally arrives at Olivia's house, in time to back up Viola against the accusations of Antonio. Olivia rejects the Duke's love: enraged, he threatens Cesario, but it is too late. Sebastian turns up and all becomes clear. Viola, united with the Duke, asks for the Captain to be set free. Olivia, married to Sebastian, will be Orsino's sister. A letter from Malvolio gains his release. All is well, and the stage is left to Feste.

Who? What? Why? Where? How?

1 To Viola, the man who rescued her from the duel. To Orsino, a 'notable pirate.' To Sebastian, a dear refound friend 5,1

2 Malvolio 5,1

3 Sebastian's life, and also his love 'without retention or restraint' 5,1

4 The 'old tune' of Orsino's wooing. The music is Cesario's 5,1

5 He has been put in prison at Malvolio's request 5,1

6 That she is a kinsman. That he is a ghost 5,1

7 In 'recompense' for writing the letter which ensnared Malvolio 5,1

8 First, not to mar the happiness of the time. Second, because there is fault on both sides 5,1

9 To follow his master the Duke, who is leaving in a rage – even if the Duke will kill him 5,1

10 They refer to a brother/sister of the same name. Their father(s) have the same name, 'both' have a mole on the brow and 'both' died when Viola was thirteen years old 5,1

Who said that?

1 Viola/Cesario 5,1

2 Olivia – to urge Cesario to be bold (he 'is' her husband). In fact, what he 'is', nobody yet knows! 5,1

3 Antonio 5,1

4 Duke Orsino 5,1

5 Malvolio 5,1

Open quotes

1 'That very envy and the tongue of loss/Cried fame and honour on him.' 5,1

2 'I'll sacrifice the lamb that I do love/To spite a raven's heart within a dove' 5,1

3 'One face, one voice, one habit and two persons.' 5,1

4 'You shall from this time be/Your master's mistress.' 5,1

5 'How with a sportful malice it was follow'd./May rather pluck on laughter than revenge.' 5,1

About time

1 Three months 5,1

2 Less than half an hour 5,1

3 Two hours 5,1

4 'The whirligig of time' 5,1

5 'Golden time' 5,1

Knots and unravellings

Antonio accuses Viola of ingratitude because she denied him and his purse, when he thought she was Sebastian. She claims mistaken identity, backed up by the Duke – because he knows nothing of Sebastian's existence, and knows that Cesario has been with him for months.

Olivia accuses Viola of a broken promise because she thinks she is Sebastian, who has in fact missed their appointment: we find out why when Sir Andrew and Sir Toby turn up and accuse Viola of beating them. (Sebastian later apologises for this.)

The Duke accuses Viola (quite rightly, as it happens) of winning Olivia's affections instead of wooing her on his behalf. With less justice, he then accuses her of dissembling because he thinks Cesario has married Olivia, a fact mistakenly affirmed by both Olivia and the Priest. In fact, of course, it is Sebastian who has married Olivia.

▣ Quotations you should know

The following quotations repeat some of the important lines that reflect aspects
of the play, its characterisation and plot.

Music

Music

Orsino introduces two of the major themes in the play, music
and love. He demonstrates his own unbalanced view of love:

'If music be the food of love, play on,
Give me excess of it, that, surfeiting,
The appetite may sicken, and so die.'

1, 3, 1–3

Orsino also voices some of the most beautiful lines in praise of
music:

'That strain again! It had a dying fall.
O, it came oe'r my ear like the sweet sound
That breathes upon a bank of violets,
Stealing and giving odour!'

1, 1, 4–7

Sebastian

Sebastian

The Captain praises Sebastian and throws light on his
character:

'...I saw your brother,
Most provident in peril, bind himself –
Courage and hope both teaching him the practice – '
1, 2, 21

Sir Toby Belch

Sir Toby

Sir Toby on the pleasures of life:

'What a plague means my niece to take the death of her
brother thus? I am sure care's an enemy to life.'

1, 3, 1

Sir Andrew Aguecheek

Maria on Sir Andrew's character:

'...he's a fool, he's a great quarreller...he hath the gift of a coward'

1, 3, 27

Viola

Viola recognises she has a problem when she falls in love with Orsino:

'I'll do my best
To woo your lady. Yet a barful strife!
Whoe'er I woo, myself would be his wife'

1, 4, 41

Orsino

Olivia comments on Orsino:

'Yet I suppose him virtuous, know him noble,
Of great estate, of fresh and stainless youth,
In voices well divulged, free, learned, and valiant,
And in dimension and the shape of nature
A gracious person.'

1, 5, 247–251

Love

Viola tells how a lover should act, and entrances Olivia:

'Make me a willow cabin at your gate,
And call upon my soul within the house;
Write loyal cantons of contemned love
And sing them loud even in the dead of night;
Hallow your name to the reverberate hills
And make the babbling gossip of the air
Cry out 'Olivia!...'

1, 5, 257–263

Olivia declares her love for 'Cesario':

'Cesario, by the roses of the spring,
By maidenhood, honour, truth and every thing,
I love thee so, that, maugre all thy pride,
Nor wit nor reason can my passion hide.'

3, 1, 161

Disguise

Disguise

Viola comments on the dangers of disguise:

'Disguise, I see thou art a wickedness,
Wherein the pregnant enemy does much.
How easy is it for the proper-false
In women's waxen hearts to set their forms!'

2, 2, 27–30

Malvolio

Malvolio

Maria's letter promises greatness to Malvolio:

'Some are born great, some achieve greatness, and
some have greatness thrust upon 'em!'

2, 5, 140

Feste

Feste

Viola on the skills of foolery and Feste:

'This fellow is wise enough to play the fool;
And to do that well craves a kind of wit.'

3, 1, 58

Olivia

Olivia

Viola says of Olivia, commenting on her haughtiness:
'I see you what you are, you are too proud;
But, if you were the devil, you are fair.'

1, 5, 269

Disorder

Disorder

Malvolio tries, unsuccessfully, to quieten Sir Toby's revelry:
'My masters, are you mad? or what are you? Have you
no wit, manners, nor honesty but to gabble like tinkers
at this time of night?'

2, 3, 92

Writing an examination essay

Take the following to heart

- *Carefully study each of the questions set on a particular text* Make sure you understand what they are asking for so that you select the one you know most about.
- *Answer the question* Obvious, isn't it? But bitter experience shows that many students fail because they do not actually answer the question that has been set.
- *Answer all the question* Again, obvious, but so many students spend all their time answering just part of a question and ignoring the rest. This prevents you gaining marks for the parts left out.

The question

1 Read and understand every word of it. If it asks you to compare (the similarities) and/or contrast (the differences) between characters or events, then that is what you must do.
2 Underline all the key words and phrases that mention characters, events and themes, and all instructions as to what to do, e.g. compare, contrast, outline, comment, give an account, write about, show how/what/where.
3 Now write a short list of the things you have to do, one item under the other. A typical question will only have between two and five items at most for you to cope with.

Planning your answer

1 Look at each of the points you have identified from the question. Think about what you are going to say about each. Much of it will be pretty obvious, but if you think of any good ideas, jot them down before you forget them.
2 Decide in what order you are going to deal with the question's major points. Number them in sequence.
3 So far you have done some concentrated, thoughtful reading and written down maybe fifteen to twenty words. You know roughly what you are going to say in response to the question and in what order – if you do not, you have time to give serious thought to trying one of the other questions.

Putting pen to paper

The first sentences are important. Try to summarise your response to the question so the examiner has some idea of how you are going to approach it. Do not say 'I am going to write about the character of Macbeth and show how evil he was' but instead write 'Macbeth was a weak-willed, vicious traitor. Totally dominated by his "fiend-like queen" he deserved the epitaph "this dead butcher" – or did he?' Jump straight into the essay, do not nibble at its extremities for a page and a half. High marks will be gained by the candidate who can show he or she has a mind engaged with the text. Your personal response is rewarded – provided you are answering the question!

As you write your essay *constantly refer back to your list of points* and make sure you are actually responding to them.

How long should it be?

There is no 'correct' length. What you must do is answer the question set, fully and sensitively in the time allowed. Allocate time to each question according to the percentage of marks awarded of it.

How much quotation or paraphrase?

Use only that which is relevant and contributes to the quality and clarity of your answer. Padding is a waste of your time and gains not a single mark.